Communities
in Globalization

D0981511

Communities in Globalization

The Invisible Mayan Nahual

Juan Pablo Pérez Sáinz and
Katharine E. Andrade-Eekhoff

ROWMAN & LITTLEFIELD PUBLISHERS, INC.
Lanham • *Boulder* • *New York* • *Toronto* • *Oxford*

ROWMAN & LITTLEFIELD PUBLISHERS, INC.

Published in the United States of America
by Rowman & Littlefield Publishers, Inc.
A Member of the Rowman & Littlefield Publishing Group
4501 Forbes Boulevard, Suite 200, Lanham, Maryland 20706
www.rowmanlittlefield.com

PO Box 317
Oxford
OX2 9RU, UK

British Library Cataloguing in Publication Information Available

Library of Congress Cataloging-in-Publication Data

Pérez Sáinz, Juan Pablo.
  Communities in globalization : the invisible mayan Nahual / Juan Pablo
Pérez Sáinz and Katharine Andrade-Eekhoff.
     p. cm.
Includes bibliographical references and index.
  ISBN 0-7425-2800-6 (cloth : alk. paper) — ISBN 0-7425-2801-4 (pbk. :
alk. paper)
  1. Central America—Economic conditions—1979– 2. Globalization. I.
Andrade-Eekhoff, Katharine. II. Title.
  HC141.P462 2003
  303.48'2728—dc21
                                                        2003011861

Printed in the United States of America

♾ ™ The paper used in this publication meets the minimum requirements of
American National Standard for Information Sciences—Permanence of Paper
for Printed Library Materials, ANSI/NISO Z39.48-1992.

Contents

Tables

Acknowledgments

We would like to thank those who have contributed to this text. Eric Hershberg, Guillermo Lathrop, Frederick Wherry, and an anonymous reviewer receive our thanks for pertinent comments on previous drafts, but we are fully responsible for the contents. The immediate predecessors of this text can be found in the results from two regional projects permitting the initial systemization of the community analysis. Ingrid Faulhaber, of the Mexico City Ford Foundation office, had the vision to understand the importance of the issues and facilitate the funding to carry out these projects. At the same time, our respective institutions, FLACSO Costa Rica and FLACSO El Salvador, have given us support, especially in the persons of our previous directors, Rafael Menjivar and Héctor Dada.

This text is the culmination of a long trajectory of research involving the support of various colleagues who helped carry out diverse studies throughout the 1990s. Hoping that we have not left anyone out, we wish to thank Maribel Carrera, Allen Cordero, Angela Leal, Elba López, Edith Olivares, and Cecilia Sanchez. We also wish to thank Nury Benavides and Leonardo Villegas for their assistance with the map and a myriad of other details. Matt Hammon and Kärstin Painter provided invaluable guidance through the process of review and editing this text for publication. Juan Pablo Pérez Sáinz owes a great debt to María Elena Montenegro, a natural practitioner in community development, especially in the area of tourism. Numerous conversations concerning the analytical proposals and the empirical results were confronted with on the ground experience, becoming a priceless gift to this text. Katharine Andrade-Eekhoff relied on the

Acknowledgments

continual support of Oscar Andrade, as well as the accompaniment and patient understanding of Misael, Daniel, and Rebeca.

But the biggest thanks go to the people in each of the communities. Without their collaboration, this text never would have materialized. We hope to be able to reciprocate their generous collaboration. In the middle of 2000, workshops were carried out in La Fortuna, San Pedro Sacatepéquez, and La Palma where the results and several proposals for action were presented to representatives of the communities. The dialogues that developed in these encounters were an opportunity to validate our analysis in that the community actors recognized our discourse.

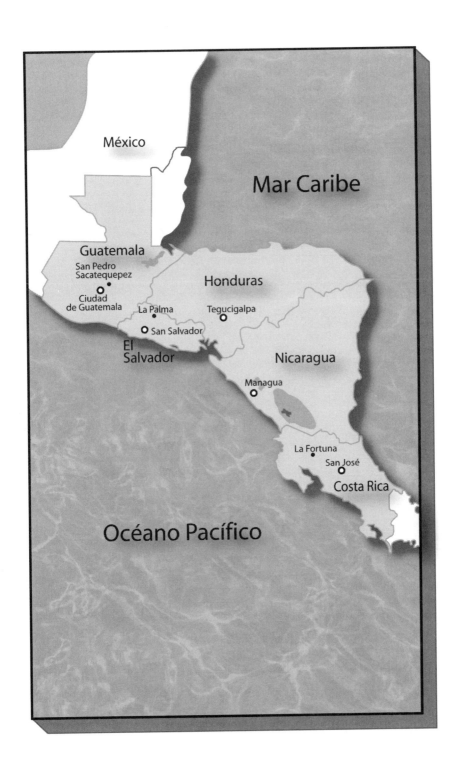

México

Mar Caribe

Guatemala

San Pedro
Sacatequepez

Honduras

Ciudad
de Guatemala   La Palma   Tegucigalpa

San Salvador

El
Salvador

Nicaragua

Managua

La Fortuna

San José

Costa Rica

Océano Pacífico

Introduction

The myth of the Nahual is an important element of the Mayan cosmo-vision, especially in the case of the Maya K'iché of Guatemala. *Nahual* refers to the transformation of human beings into animals in order to carry out actions that would not be possible in human form. The *Popol Vuh*, the holy book and cosmogonic story of this people, contains examples. The famous hero twins, Hunahpú and Ixbalanqué, transform into different beings in order to defeat the lords of death, Xibalbá, and expel them from the world of humans. Another mythic transformation is told in the battle of Pedro de Alvarado, conqueror of Guatemala, waged in roughly 1524 against Tecún Uman, who led the K'iché warriors. In his duel with Alvarado, Tecún turns into a *quetzal*, the mythic bird of the Mayan world, in order to defend himself from the conqueror. In the end, Tecún dies when pierced by Alvarado's lance. In this case, the Nahual was not strong enough to overcome the danger of the Spanish conquest. In these communities today, the Nahual is known as a spirit or an animal that accompanies and protects one from the day one is born until the day one dies.

This text is not about the Mayan myth, but does refer to it metaphorically. This book is about other dangers and threats (to livelihoods, to well-being, to community, etc.) from today's world, evident in the exclusionary tendencies of the phenomenon called globalization, a new Alvarado with an even more powerful lance. The threatened communities are those that have until recently been called the Third World, facing tendencies that can send them into the Other World. (*Other World* here refers metaphorically to death or inexistence—the nonhuman world.) Mostly, this book seeks to

1

identify the resources of these communities that will allow them to face globalization while minimizing the risks and maximizing their opportunities. This potential is what we see as the community's Nahual. To be able to transform into the Nahual, and thereby activate these resources, could prevent exclusion from the globalized world. It is in this way that the Mayan world guides us metaphorically through our analytical argument, as we outline below.

Globalization is one of the most (ab)used terms in the social sciences today. In fact, it has been the center of great debates at the end of the twentieth century and the beginning of this one. Practically any phenomenon considered innovative is interpreted through or refers to this notion, and because of its indiscriminate use, its heuristic value is placed in danger.[1] This text does not lay forth yet another definition and characterization of this process but rather concentrates on one of the principal paradoxes indicative of its contradictory character. Intuitively, the term *globalization* suggests ideas such as the compression of the world, or the development of a planetary consciousness, or the negation of space by time minimizing physical distances between places. In this sense, we might consider that we face a process of homogenization on a worldwide scale. However, empirical evidence shows that numerous places have come to the forefront, setting about an authentic revitalization of the local. This has led to a curious neologism in English: "glocalization" (Swygendouw 1992; Robertson 1995). It is this paradox that interests us and opens the doors to the reflections in this book.

The revitalization of the local, in the context of globalization, has led to a copious bibliography. Despite this, however, some notable analytical lagoons denote the way in which the global market has imposed itself on the local. This vision prioritizes the local as a space that brings together competing businesses in this market and of institutions that provide conditions for governance. In other words, and forcing the argument, the local is basically understood as a functional territory for global accumulation materialized by firms. This text places itself far from that perspective. Rather, we emphasize three issues that the mainstream has placed on a back burner, if not all together ignored.

First, we stress the importance of a certain type of territory, relevant to societies in the South, which has received insufficient attention in the accumulated knowledge on the topic precisely because most empirical references are from the North.[2] Because of this, the globalized locale has been fundamentally understood as one of two types of socioterritories: the first is that of globalized cities, and the second refers to winning regions. In thinking about Latin America—and, more concretely, Central America, where our empirical references are located—we have major doubts as to whether global cities can be discussed. It is difficult to identify an urban

center in the region that meets all of the following conditions: being a location for transnational firms carrying out strategic activities (design,
innovation, marketing, etc.); being an important financial center (the
hegemonic form of global capital); having a relevant presence of foreign
immigrant labor; having a concentration of the intellectual elite who provide cultural prestige to the city; and constituting an important international tourist destination. Neither Mexico City nor São Paulo (much less
Buenos Aires, given the current crisis) meets all of these conditions.
The region is different given that important transformations have taken
place in Latin America, fundamentally in two arenas. On the one hand,
there has been a shift in the mode of accumulation, which has meant in
some cases a modification of territories where urban areas, especially metropolitan ones, are no longer the privileged spaces for capital accumulation.
At the same time, state decentralization, a key component of structural adjustment policies applied in Latin America, opens up possibilities for new
regional development. In other words, the region appears as a local socioterritory that is relevant in Latin America's insertion in globalization.
But this text recovers another type of local socioterritory that we consider to be important for the South but that these types of studies have not
reclaimed: that of the neighborhood community. The term refers to Tonnies's ([1957] 1996) classic typology of communities: blood, neighborhood, and spiritual. Without going into a discussion of the pertinence of
this typology, we consider that the second is of great analytical relevance
for broaching the revitalization of the local in globalization. It suggests the
existence of a space with links that are based in a territory, thereby generating community belonging. Obviously its economic base cannot be
limited to agriculture, as the German author argued in his time; rather,
nonagricultural, artisan, and even manufacturing and services can be produced within it. This diversity is precisely a result of the new geography
of globalization. In fact, the empirical references used in this text and explained in more detail later do not refer to any agricultural activity. The
revitalization of the neighborhood community as a socioterritory implies
a redefinition of the space of the previous modernizing period that laid
out the classic distinction between rural/urban, also coinciding with that
of agrarian/nonagrarian, and it refers to a deep distinction between tradi-
tional/modern. Today, with globalization, rural areas do not necessarily
have to be predominately agrarian and cannot be reduced to what is considered traditional.
Second, recovering this local socioterritory implies reclaiming the community as an actor in globalization. This in turn implies questioning the
practically exclusive protagonism of businesses, especially multinational
firms, as the actor in globalization. Indeed, transnational migration
demonstrates that this process is not always part of a business strategy or

related public policy. Rather, these flows are a societal response and imply modes of insertion in the globalizing process that differ from those
that originate from the economy or state. While migration is familiar in
origin, its viability through networks tends toward collectivization and
can lead to processes that involve entire communities, as can be found, for
example, in collective remittances. It is in this sense that transnational
communities are now spoken of, and it demonstrates that communities
can be actors in globalization as well. But community protagonism is not
reduced to the phenomenon of transnational migration. Communities can
be inserted into globalization in other scenarios, such as tourism, including handicraft production, new agricultural exports, or manufacturing
subcontracting, among others. These types of situations are not generally
considered in the mainstream bibliography and thus remain hidden. Re-
vealing them is a fundamental part of the critical challenge assumed in
this text.
    The third issue that we want to emphasize has to do with the dimen-
sion of equity in the process of community insertion in globalization.
Mainstream references on globalized locales tend to emphasize economic
or political dimensions. The economic dimension refers to the discussion
of local economies, structured as a cluster of activities dedicated to offering the same type of good or service in a shared territory; thus, what is
generally emphasized is the ability to compete in the global market. If this
is presented in terms of global commodity chains, in that these chains
form the structure of the new global economy, then competition is an issue of upgrading in the respective chain, and it raises the broader problem of a sustainable insertion in globalization. But this upgrading refers
only to firms and, more concretely, the efficient ones. On the other hand,
when the political dimension is emphasized, the problem that tends to be
privileged is that of political-administrative decentralization. The relevant issue is whether the decentralizing dynamic has any relationship at
all with the globalized economic dynamic. In other words, this has to do
with issues related to economic governance and whether the local institutional configuration can take advantage of the link between local economic activities and the global market. At the same time, the social
dimension, if not completely absent, emerges only peripherally as a mere
result of virtuous economic and/or political dynamics.
    In our opinion, the consideration of the equity dimension implies that up-
grading could be used as a concept to redefine the old problem of development in this new period of globalization. But the current debate concerning
this term—which faces-off positions that privilege the local through the
analysis of clusters against interpretations that privilege the global based on
global commodity chains—cannot be ignored. To relate our own point of
view, it is important to briefly outline the basic coordinates of this argument.[3]

The current reflection about clusters already has a history of debate dating back several decades, initiated with the analysis of industrial districts, especially those of Italy. But the reification of the Italian model led to its abandonment. In fact, its use as a Weberian ideal type resulted in a nondynamic conception which, what's more, was closed off to cultural specifics, about which it is difficult to generalize, especially in developing countries (Bair and Gereffi 2001). In this way, an analytical concept of great potential was lost, but one that we hope to recover in this book: that of the socioterritory (Becattini 1992).[4] This relative loss of sociocultural factors, such as local embeddedness, has meant that the analysis tends to privilege the relationships between firms losing a wider vision of the whole of the socioterritory. This change is clear with the arrival of the concept of collective efficiency that adds to Marshall's concept of external economies, emerging with the idea of joint action (cooperation among firms and the formation of business associations) (Schmitz 1995, 1999). Thus, a second moment of the reflection is inaugurated where this analytical framework is applied to examples predominantly in developing countries. Schmitz and Nadvi (1999) have precisely synthesized the principal findings of these studies. First, the experience of clusters in these countries is significant and thus relevant as a topic related to development. Second, the experiences are quite diverse and differ from the Italian model. Third, internal differentiation, in terms of distinct types of firms, is significant. In this way there are similarities with the Italy of the 1990s but not with that of the 1970s or even the 1980s. Finally, because it is difficult to refer to the Italian model, a more dynamic analytical perspective based on the notion of trajectory as outlined by Humphrey (1995) was proposed instead. However, two weaknesses are recognized in this reflection. On the one hand, external links are not sufficiently captured. On the other, external challenges require more economic governance than that implied by joint action; in other words, institutionality becomes a fundamental question in terms of upgrading the respective cluster.

It is precisely these weaknesses that become strengths for those foci that privilege the global based on an understanding of the world economy in terms of global commodity chains. Without a doubt, the key author here is Gereffi (Gereffi and Korzeniewicz 1994; Gereffi 1995; Gereffi and Hamilton 1996). For this author and his numerous followers, the issue of upgrading lies in the sort of relationship that exists between firms that control the chain with local firms. This thesis has been recently and convincingly argued in the study of Bair and Gereffi (2001) in Torreón, a northern locale in Mexico that has become the "world capital" of jeans. The strategies followed by several of the leading firms in the chain are what explain the ability of certain local businesses to enter into the dynamics of upgrading, not those factors linked to the focus of collective efficiency that are glaringly absent in the Mexican locale.

Thus, we can see two postures in the mainstream reflections on the topic of upgrading.[5] If, metaphorically speaking, upgrading is understood as an action of climbing the rungs of the globalization ladder, the focus based on clusters would argue that the impulse comes from below by a group of local firms with sufficient institutionality. The other focus would point toward upgrading strategies that originate from above, with the leading global firms incorporating their local counterparts. Maybe both are right because they are talking about different ladders. In other words, there is not just one ladder in globalization but rather several. In this sense, it is interesting to refer to one of the more recent studies concerning shoe chains, carried out by two well-known authors from the cluster focus (Schmitz and Knorringa 2000). But their analytical view has focused on the global purchasing firms, as in the global commodity chain focus. What is interesting in this study is that two types of trajectories are identified. The first is based on old clusters, largely the fruit of endogenous processes. However, the foundation of the second is in new clusters, externally induced by global firms. We consider that the analytical pertinence of the cluster focus corresponds to the first type, while the explanations of Gereffi and others are more relevant in the second type of situation. Regardless, insinuated in this later situation, is that as upgrading advances, global firms become the main protagonists. In fact, Humphrey and Schmitz (1998) have argued that with the development of the cluster, the local cohesive factors, especially trust, tend to disappear and external actors become more relevant. In other words, maybe the two ladders converge, and the ladder of Gereffi and associates becomes longer.

We, however, wish to explore a third ladder, even though this text, because it refers to the experience of configuring a cluster that has not been induced by global firms, should frame itself in the first focus outlined in the preceding paragraphs. However, there is a fundamental difference from that of clusters. Due to the three issues that we have identified as crucial and that have been devalued in the mainstream interpretations, upgrading, as we see it, should not be limited to the cluster but rather applied to the community as a whole. This implies that the trajectory does not necessarily have to weaken the local elements (the sociocultural and political-institutional context) and bring about the predominance of the global (leading firms in globalization). If history has taught us anything in the last few years, it is to be suspect of any teleological proposal; in other words, we suspect that there are multiple trajectories. If community upgrading is not possible, upgrading in globalization cannot be synonymous with development. Firms do not guarantee sufficient equity even when leading global firms abide by codes of conduct, however ethical or politically correct. Thus, if upgrading is limited to a process of increasing competitiveness of specific firms or an agglomerated group of them, this term cannot redefine the problem of development. This implies that this phenomenon and globalization are incompatible. We consider this to be too radical to be true.

It is true that, in comparison with the national modernization context, today it is much more difficult to determine what constitutes development. As an approximation of this tremendously elusive term, we understand it to be a production process of goods and services, accessible to the majority of the members of a community who establish mechanisms, according to certain standards of equity, for distribution of the fruits of this production.[6] However, the majority of these defining elements are very difficult to pinpoint. The boundaries of a community are even less precise than those of a nation that has borders defined by the state, even if they are imagined. And we would venture that access takes place not through the means of production, as in days gone by, but fundamentally through knowledge, which is an intangible resource. Additionally, equity not only has a persistent class dimension but incorporates multiple dimensions. But these analytical difficulties of definition that turn into modes for intervention in the political arena do not mean that development is impossible in globalization. We believe that this possibility does exist, but as always, it is relative. History, which enjoys good health and is far from ending, offers multiple paths; some are just too surprising for us to grasp.

Because of this, this book proposes as an analytical starting point the issue of equity, which consequently impacts the manner in which the other two dimensions are approached. Thus, the obsession with competitiveness, characterizing a good number of studies, is redefined in terms of the cohesion of the respective cluster. In this way, the cluster should be more than simply a gathering of businesses sharing the same activity and territory. External economies and different modes of community capital are fundamental elements in obtaining this cohesion. But what is important in this phenomenon is that the upgrading in the global market is not an attribute of a few firms but rather of the entire cluster and, ultimately, a community process. In this way, the social angle of development can be recovered, and upgrading can be redefined as development in the current globalizing process. As far as the political dimension, equity presents the need to constitute an arena for coordinating efforts where consensus can be reached and a new community contract can be (re)defined in the context of globalization. In other words, equity is not just an effect of the type of global insertion but should also be a condition for this integration. Tell me about equity in your community, and I will tell you how your upgrading will be in the global market.

The reflections in the preceding paragraphs imply that this text will take on a three-dimensional analytical framework. First, it seeks to make community experiences of global insertion visible, where neither large multinational firms nor state policies have played an important role. Thus, as reflected in the title of this book, we have added the adjective *invisible* to the metaphor of the Nahual. Second, it presents a view of globalization from the local, emphasizing the local conditions for upgrading. And third, the starting point for this analysis is equity so that economic and political processes incorporate the upgrading of not just a few but of the community as a whole. The centrality of the community and its potential are what we have attempted to demonstrate with the metaphor of the Nahual.

These issues have concerned us for over ten years, since we carried out the first study in San Pedro Sacatepéquez, Guatemala, an indigenous community near the capital, inserted in global production chains of apparel manufacturing through subcontracting. This study was part of a regional project directed by Alejandro Portes. The community was selected because it provided an example of a universe of dynamic microenterprises. Additionally, Portes had begun to delve into the concept of social capital, providing an analytical framework that has been fundamental in the trajectory of research projects carried out since then and that is reflected in this text. However, as we will argue in the following pages, we have decided to substitute the term *social capital* for that of *community capital*.[7] Other studies followed the first one in different communities as well as revisiting some of the same places. During the last decade, studies have been carried out in fifteen communities, with diverse insertions in globalization, in locales throughout Central America (Pérez Sáinz 1999a; Pérez Sáinz and Andrade-Eekhoff 1999; Pérez Sáinz et al. 2001). Since 1998, thanks to the support of the Mexico City office of the Ford Foundation, two regional research projects were carried out in several communities, allowing for a systematization of the analysis. This book uses only three of the empirical references from this decade of regional research projects, but obviously it gathers the accumulated knowledge from a trajectory of investigations leading to a consolidated systemization.

The following pages develop the analysis in the three locales that constitute our empirical reference points. They correspond to different scenarios of interaction between the local and the global identified in Central America. Thus, there is the scenario of tourism analyzed through the experiences of La Fortuna in Costa Rica, which has become one of the principal international tourist destination in this country. San Pedro Sacatepéquez serves as the manufacturing subcontracting site for the apparel industry and constitutes one of the most fascinating cases of insertion in globalization of an indigenous community from the region. The third case is La Palma in El Salvador, where handicrafts are produced; this community is recognized as the emblematic craft producer for the country.

This selection corresponds to two basic criteria. First, these are the cases about which we have accumulated more knowledge, since at least two studies have been carried out in each locale, allowing for a certain diachronic perspective on these places. Second, they are prominent examples of their respective scenarios, as has already been mentioned. However, while they are considered successful cases, they are not without problems. So they are examples that help show that globalization offers communities a dialectical play between threats and opportunities.

While these empirical references are located in Central America, we believe that the neighborhood community, with clustered activities in the global marketplace, is an object of study that transcends the limits of this region. We are sure that the reflections developed in this book will be useful for the study of community realities in other latitudes of the planet. Part of the new geography of globalization, beyond that imposed by multinational firms, are those scenarios of interaction between the local and the global incorporating neighborhood communities. So it does not seem far-fetched for us to suggest that there might be more affinity between La Fortuna and a tourist community, for example, in the Philippines than that which might exist with many rural locales in Costa Rica oriented, for example, to the production of basic grains for the internal market. The same could be said of similarities between La Palma and a multitude of handicraft communities around the globe that share the same difficulties of insertion, in a nonprecarious way, in the global market. And we are sure that there will be readers who recognize in their own country communities similar to that of San Pedro Sacatepéquez. In other words, this is an issue with universalizing veneers, and the selection of these Central American cases does not mean that we are broaching an issue pertinent only to this region.

This book has four chapters. The first contextualizes the discussion in two ways. First, it presents the analytical pertinence of the neighborhood community as a local socioterritory in the discussion concerning the revitalization of the local in globalization. Second, it offers an outline of the scenarios of interaction between the local and the global in Central America.

Chapter 2 starts with a description of the three case studies that serve as empirical reference points for the reflection discussing the genesis of the insertion of each locale in the globalizing process. This chapter demonstrates our methodological preference since the analysis of the local begins with the issue of equity. Here the material welfare of the households and their determining factors are analyzed first. This is followed by an analysis of the social dynamics in the labor market. With this understanding of the sociolabor issues, we return to the households and present a holistic view of local dynamics in order to identify important topics to be addressed in the following chapter.

The third chapter considers three key issues. The first has to do with the cluster of the globalized activity. Heterogeneity and external economies are the topics that are analyzed. These then refer us to the issue of the cohesion of the cluster that has not only a sectoral dimension, referred to as external economies, but also a socioterritorial one where community capital is the fundamental question. The last issue of this chapter has to do with the political-institutional dynamics of the locales.

The fourth and final chapter of the analysis has three parts. The first relates to the articulation of the communities with the global market where the issues of global commodity chains and upgrading are the key factors. Second, based on all elements, both internal as well as external, we attempt to offer a holistic vision of each community facing globalization, emphasizing the opportunities and risks in each. The chapter ends with an attempt to offer an analytical framework of local dynamics in globalization, with heuristic as well as normative pretenses. This analytical proposal transcends Central America and the universes studied, in that we believe, as we have already argued, that we are facing a set of broader more universal problems.

The end of the book includes a methodological appendix that offers details of the fieldwork carried out.

We hope with this publication that we can influence the common sense of policymakers. Our dream would be that they are able to visualize these experiences and appreciate the dialectical play between threats and opportunities for the insertion of these types of locales in globalization so that more beneficial interventions can be designed for the communities.

NOTES

1. We should not be surprised that this has led to a true inflation of metaphors (Ianni 1998).

2. It can be said that this distinction, which refers to countries, is obsolete in terms of the new geography of globalization. However, as it will be argued in this text, the nation, while having lost its centrality, has not disappeared, and belonging to a country impacts the local even in globalization.

3. It is important to mention that this debate takes places in terms of one type of global commodity chains: those that are buyer driven. This type of situation is more relevant for the realities that concern us here.

4. As is clear; we have already used the term.

5. The term *upgrading* has been accompanied by the adjective *industrial,* which imposes a limitation on the concept, reducing it to manufacturing activities with-

out taking into account agrarian and, more important in the global economy, service activities. However, as will be shown in this text, there have been attempts to apply this concept to nonmanufacturing activities. But its even greater limitation is confining it to the world of businesses without further consideration of social aspects.

6. What is produced, how it is accessed, and how it is distributed change according to the historical context.

7. This term, as will be developed in the third chapter, is understood as the individual appropriation of community resources that are sociocultural in nature by business owners in the respective cluster whose effects bring about cohesion within the cluster.

Equity: Impartiality — value of a property or of an interest in it in excess of claims against it.

Trajectory — the curve that a body describes in space.

Heterogeneity — Mixed

1

The Global
and the Local

A s mentioned in the introduction, this first chapter serves a dual pur-
pose. The first is theoretical in nature and seeks to recoup the significance of the neighborhood community as an expression of the local in
societies such as those in Central America within the revitalization of this
type of territory occurring in globalization. Second, we outline the new
scenarios emerging in the region related with the dynamics of globalization to show that certain types of communities can insert into these forces.
In this way, we seek to validate, for Central America, the arguments
placed forth in the first section of this chapter. These two objectives are
taken up in separate sections.

GLOBALIZATION AND COMMUNITY:
SOME THEORETICAL REFLECTIONS

The intuitive idea of globalization, as a compression of the world, refers
to the issue of the construction of time and space in modernity. In this
regard, Giddens (1994) considers that the separation of time from
space,[1] along with the development of the mechanisms of unanchoring
(the separating of social activity from its localized contexts) and the reflexive appropriation of knowledge, is one of the three great sources of
modernity. This separation took place through two mechanisms. On the
one hand, the clock supposed the uniformity of the measurement of
time and disconnected it from its associated space. On the other hand,
the separation between place (understood as the geographic materiality

of social activity) and space brought about interactions between absentees giving place a phantasmagoric meaning.[2] According to Giddens, this double separation is vital for modern dynamics for three reasons. First, it makes the unanchoring mechanism possible, another of the other primary sources of modernization as mentioned. Second, the rationalized organization of society is produced. Third, it allows for a radical historicity of modernity itself.

Giddens's reflections—concretely, the mechanisms of time and space separation—can be reinterpreted in terms of the processes of abstraction resulting from the generalization of commodity production characteristic of capitalist modernity.[3] Marx (1975) is the classic author to recoup here with perhaps the most brilliant pages of his masterpiece, those referring to the abstraction of labor, providing the foundation for his theory of exploitation and alienation. The abstract time (of labor) is a product of this mercantile generalization associated with modernity, and it can be argued that the loss of the signs of concrete labor is also an abstraction, resulting in the subsequent loss of the territorial conditions of production. But these abstractions of time and space, and their corollary of separation between both, have taken place within a certain historic process. Regarding this point, Harvey (1989) has identified three important moments in not just a material plane but also a symbolic one in terms of perceptions of time and space: 1847–1948, the dawn of World War I and the last two decades of the last century. It is this last period that particularly concerns us given that it places us in the historical moment of globalization.

Concerning the globalization phenomenon and its consequences in terms of the split between space and time, there are two key issues to highlight. On the one hand, the new transformations in communication have had even more profound impacts than those at the end of the nineteenth century. The new technological revolution has implied, among other things, radical changes in the areas of transportation and communication that make relative the classic coordinates of space and time (Cerny 1995; Gereffi 1995). On the other hand, the volatility of markets of goods— and, more important, financial markets—must be highlighted. It is in this final aspect that an authentic "dematerialization" of exchange (Lash and Urry 1993) has taken place, generating a growing split between this immaterial world and that of material exchanges in the real economy. In other words, a "virtualization" of the economy has taken place (Sassen 1996). This has been possible because financial globalization represents perhaps the most consumed expression of technological development in the field of communications (Cerny 1995).

In terms of time, the globalizing impact has meant that simultaneity becomes instant, and, as a result, space appears to have been annulled and is therefore irrelevant. This in turn produces "nonplaces" that are precisely the highest expression of opposition between space and place (Augé 1996). In this sense, virtual space is a genuinely constituted territory of globalization, of which the already mentioned financial markets would be emblematic. According to Harvey (1989), this new compression is what makes possible the simulacrum of reality since world geography can be experienced, indirectly, through multiple daily activities (from eating to entertainment).

However, one has to be careful not to fall into the temptation of believing that this capitalist modernization process of time and space compression has been consummated. Limiting ourselves to this second element (which is the aspect that concerns us and following upon Augé [1996]), this issue can be formulated in terms of the false polarities between place (the geographic reference of modern space) and nonplace (a product of "overmodernity," using the term from this author), in the sense that the first is never completely erased, nor is the second completely constituted. Additionally, globalization has not led to the disappearance of the principal territory constituting modernity: the nation. Nonetheless, the nation, along with the state, has suffered important transformations due to globalization that deserve mention since they will allow us to develop our proposition concerning the revival of the local in globalization.

First, globalization supposes changes in the international system.[4] In this regard, Cerny (1995) argues that this field is no longer a "system of states" but rather has been transmuted into a plural and complex structure called *plurilateral*. The state loses primacy as a unifying actor of the international system. This loss can also be expressed as deterritorialization. Concerning this, Appadurai (1996) has pointed to the constitution of different types of global "scapes": ethnic (movement of migrants, tourists, refugees, etc.); technical (flows of technical knowledge); financial (transactions of the virtual economy); of communications and media (instantaneous distribution of merchandise, global consumerism, etc.); and of ideas (universalization of the Western cosmology of modernity). What is important is the increasing disjuncture between them. This phenomenon is one of the principal causes, as far as this author is concerned, that the hyphen that unites the terms *nation* with *state* is losing its function as an icon of conjunction, indicating rather its disjunction.[5]

However, these perceptions need to be made relative by introducing a rather convincing argument denominated by the skeptics',[6] view of globalization. This perspective argues that national sovereignty remains quite permanent in terms of control of the population, since the international mobility of the labor force, while it exists, is much less than that of capital (Hirst and Thompson 1996).[7] In this regard, we identify ourselves with the more balanced approach of Sassen (1996) in arguing that globalization has decentered sovereignty and partially denationalized territory. In other words, sovereignty and territory continue to be essential elements of the international system, implying that the nation-state continues to make up this system, but without the same level of determination as in the past.

Second, the crisis of the Fordist model of regulation of capitalism, imposed fundamentally in advanced capitalist societies after World War II, has had important effects on the state and its national space. One of the fundamental elements of this model[8] must be remembered: the conformation of a monopolistic regulationist mode where real wage increases followed those of productivity based on institutional arrangements that were national in scope (state, unions, social security system, etc.). In other words, the constitution and exercise of a social state take place in the framework of the nation-state (Castel 1997). In this way, the increases in production, especially those related to consumer durables, were absorbed by the increase in actual demand, guaranteeing the link between production and reproduction within national space based on social contracts.[9]

However, this regulation also had to be transnationally guaranteed given the internationalization of capital, accented toward the end of the nineteenth century. The Bretton Woods agreement of 1944, establishing an international financial system based on the U.S. dollar, was the backbone of the institutional arrangement at this level. But it should be emphasized that the regulation rested fundamentally on the framework of the nation-state (Amin 1994). However, both forms of regulation (national and international) entered into contradiction. The configuration of the social contract was diverse since it responded to national specificities; in other words, different types of social contracts were generated, allowing for differing conditions for the accumulation of capital in each national reality. This differentiation inevitably meant that the processes of exchange of merchandise and the transnationalization of capital would deepen, and in the end has resulted in a questioning of the national framework for determining the accumulation of capital. Thus, the world economy began to be transformed, moving from a system of productive spaces with national boundaries to a fragmented system of productive and consumption spaces that do not coincide with these limits. In this way, what has come to be known as a global economy emerges where international arrangements and principally national regulations have not been able to maintain their capital reproductive function. Thus, the national social contracts of the Fordist model, and thus the social state, entered into crisis (Swygendouw 1992; Castel 1997).

The result of this process has led to the installation of what Swygendouw (1992) calls global disorder.[10] According to this author, this disorder is manifested through two basic phenomena. The first has to do with the displacement of the production of commodities with financial speculation as the principal means of accumulation. Globalization, the compression of the world, has lead to a rationale that prioritizes short-term investment over long-term. The second phenomenon refers to the adaptations assumed by productive capital, specifically in large transnational firms. In this regard, these firms confront a basic contradiction: They need to penetrate new very volatile markets, but at the same time their production continues to take place in a set space for some time. This tension was managed during the previous period through direct investment thanks to the monetary stability that the institutional arrangements allowed for. But, in this current situation of financial instability, this strategy becomes unpredictable and risky.[11]

A third phenomenon to highlight, related to the previous, is that this global disorder has nonetheless led to a set of new regulatory formations whose fundamental characteristic is its local horizon, demonstrating that regions and cities, as opposed to nation-states, are able to adapt to changes in the market, technology, and culture (Castells and Hall 1994). Various trends can be mentioned. First, the regulation of the capital-labor relationship shifts from the national arena to that of business. In fact, one of the key elements of labor flexibility is that it seeks to redefine the space of arrangements aspiring to a mere relationship between firms and individual people. Second, this displacement involves a fragmentation of the labor markets where the local conditions are elemental in the configuration. Third, the tendency toward individualization, mentioned in the regulation of labor relations, is detected also in collective consumption and can be seen in the trend of the privatization of social services. Finally, a redefinition of political space takes place where the local becomes relevant. Thus, in today's world, the local emerges as a mode of administration of the global in terms of productivity and economic competitiveness as well as sociocultural integration and representation, and political management (Borja and Castells 1997).

However, Swyngedouw (1992) is emphatic in warning that this localization of regulatory structures increases the power of capital over space. Consequently, these structures will have problems in carrying out their regulatory functions. This means that the nation-state does not disappear from the regulatory horizon.[12] Based on this, Robinson (1996) argues that the nation-state does not disappear but is transformed into a neoliberal state. And in fact, macroeconomic stability within national frameworks, something that only the state can maintain, is an essential condition for the reproduction of global capital. In fact, it has been argued that the actions of national states are the main boundary of the contexts where multinational firms operate (Dicken 1992). And, in this same way, the argument from the skeptics' viewpoint on globalization can be mentioned: the existence of various levels of "economic governance" (agreements between economic powers, international regulatory institutions, regional economic blocks, national policies, and regional policies) where the national plays a key role in articulating the supranational bodies along with those of the subnational (Hirst and Thompson 1996).

Thus, it seems reasonable to argue that the nation-state, given globalizing effects, has been subjected to important redefinitions that we would synthesize with the idea of a loss of its previous centrality. This can be seen on two levels: supranationally, with the constitution of economic blocks as an effect of the globalization of economies; and subnationally, where the local, in its distinct territorial manifestations, gains importance in terms of regulation. In other words, the nation, a space generated by the abstraction of places induced by modernity, has not disappeared, and at the same time globalization has revitalized places, showing that time has not made space null and void. As Harvey (1989) emphasizes, the central paradox is that as spatial barriers are of less importance, capital is more sensitive to variations of places within space, and thus greater are the incentives for places to differentiate themselves to attract capital. As Gray (1998) has pointed out, the global market would not have developed had salaries, infrastructure specializations, and political risks been the same in all latitudes. This final reflection places us fully in the issue that interests us: the revitalization of the local with the globalizing process and the function of its governance.[13]

This revitalization has to do with the ability of the local to articulate itself with global dynamics. Obviously, this peculiarity is not generalized and depends on how the global is embedded by locales. Here, Amin and Thrift (1993) have pointed out that the local should offer three elements: facilitate initial contacts to disseminate discourses and collective representations of globalization, allow for social and cultural interaction, and permit the development of innovations. This embeddedness can be of firms or activities that are exogenous to the locale or local businesses. Concerning local businesses, industrial districts are one of the most vigorous revitalizations of the local expressed in a socioterritoriality that combines with community (in the sense of generationally transferred shared values) and the clustering of businesses (marked by the division of labor and the absence of a concentration of firms) (Becattini 1992). But what is crucial in this embeddedness is showing that globalization also needs a sociocultural context to make it possible and that a large part of the comparative advantages of these locales resides in these types of factors. From the local perspective, this idea questions the economic discourse on globalization and invites a societal vision where different fields (economic, political, cultural, etc.) are taken into account.

The local has been fundamentally understood based on two types of socioterritories. The first is urban, and debate has centered on global cities

(Sassen 1991), technopoles (Castells and Hall 1994), or global networks of urban nodes (Borja and Castells 1997). The second is the region where the issues of the already mentioned industrial districts present the rising of a new territoriality and economic geography (Pyke, Becattini, and Sengenberger 1992; Pyke and Sengenberger 1993; Benko and Lipietz 1994) or the emergence of territorial milieu (to use the French term that this viewpoint has generated) where a system of production, actors, culture, and mainly a collective process of learning is articulated (Camagni 1991). If we begin to consider the Latin American realities, and more concretely Central America, we have doubts as to whether we can speak of global cities, taking into account the five conditions from the literature: transnational firms carrying out strategic activities (design, innovation, marketing, etc.); the development of financial markets (the hegemonic form of capital in globalization); an important presence of foreign immigrant labor; a concentration of the intellectual elite giving prestige to the city; and an important flow of international tourists (García Canclini 1999).[14] The region is different since in Latin America important changes have taken place, fundamentally for two reasons. First, the change in the model of accumulation has meant, in some cases, modifications in territories. If during the previous modernization period the territoriality of import substitution industrialization, the main accumulative axis, took place in urban areas, principally metropolitan, the new model introduces a new territorialization. This can even be nonurban, as is happening in rural areas where industrial export free trade zones are locating in several countries. This does not mean that metropolitan centers are condemned to unavoidable processes of deterioration; this depends on the capacity for conversion with the opening found in nonproductive paths such as the development of services. Second, state decentralization, a key component of structural adjustment programs applied in Latin America, opens up possibilities for new regional development. Thus, it is not strange to see a resurgence in reflections on regional issues (Panadero Moya et al. 1992; Curbelo et al. 1994; De Mattos et al. 1998; Instituto Latinoamericano y del Caribe de Planificación Económica y Social [ILPES]/Centro de Estudios Urbanos [CEUR] 1999).

But there is another level of the local that is probably more pertinent for realities such as the Central American. We are referring to the local community. Our hypothesis is that the fragmenting impact of globalization is greater in more fragile nation-states. Thus, in countries where the state has a smaller role in the process of accumulation based on import substitution industrialization and where unequal dynamics lead to little social integration, the local has more clearly emerged. The following reflections start with this premise.

We propose that the constitution of the local community is the product of a convergence of three territorial rationales. The first is what we call

historic and refers to the original configuration of the community territory. It corresponds to a premodern period and can be analyzed in the
classic terms of Tonnies (1996) as a community of place based on
the neighborhood and whose space is the town, but it should not be limited to agricultural activities, as Tonnies proposed.[15] It is fundamentally in
this sense, although not exclusively, that belonging to a territory serves as
a source of identity (Arocena 1995). Thus, identities, as well as having a
temporal axis, also have a spatial one defined by location and mobility of
the social actors in territories (Debuyst 1998).

A second rationale of territorial constitution would be the state. The
political-administrative ordering of space from the state also makes up
the local community. This rationale comes from modernization itself
within the process of the formation of the nation-state. This implies that
one cannot speak of community, in the traditional sense, as has been done
from economics, emphasizing three key characteristics: perfect information, continual interaction generating trust, and a reduced size of the community group. In fact there is full liberty to come and go from the
community, dissent from traditional authorities exists, competition criteria function, and socioeconomic differentiation takes place (Abraham and
Platteau 2000). On the other hand, this state rationale implies that locales
should incubate and reproduce national citizens and not local subjects
(Appadurai 1996).

But this logic in recent times has been affected by state reform imposed
by structural adjustment processes in Central America as well as the rest
of Latin America. The phenomenon to emphasize is administrative decentralization that seeks to strengthen the local state in detriment to the
central. The reflection on decentralization in Latin America is vast. Since
the beginning of the 1990s, as pointed out by De Mattos (1994), three cur-
rents have taken shape: the first proposes decentralization as a means for
endogenous development; the second sees it as an instrument for popular democratization; and the third emphasizes its utility in terms of capitalist restructuring. These views, as argued by Doner and Hershberg
(1999), have centered on three issues. The first has to do with the desire
to increase popular participation in public affairs. The second points
more toward increased control and accountability of local authorities.
The third refers to the provision of public services by seeking the cooperation of various actors (the state itself, multilateral agencies, the private
sector, and nongovernmental organizations [NGOs]). It is important to
highlight that these discussions have taken place within two basic parameters: (1) the transition from authoritarian regimes to liberal democ-
racies and (2) state reform imposed by structural adjustment programs.

The third rationale to consider is that induced by globalization itself in
terms of the revitalization of the local.[16] A basic typology of ideal situa-

tions can be imagined by taking into account two differentiating axes; the first has to do with whether the insertion of the community in globalization is the fruit of exogenous or endogenous processes, and the second refers to the type of central resource mobilized by the community in this insertion, differentiating between the labor force and entrepreneurial abilities.[17] These situations are reflected in table 1.1. The first cell represents the situation of the *enclave*, where there are nonlocal firms or groups of firms located in the community territory, implying that the insertion in globalization is predominantly a function of providing labor. When this resource continues to dominate but the initiative is endogenous, we face principally a situation of *transnational migration*. In the third cell, the community resource has changed, but the insertion takes place exogenously; we have called this situation *subcontracting*, which should not be limited to manufacturing but can also involve agrarian or service activities. Finally, when entrepreneurship is the principal resource and the insertion is endogenous, we face what we call *local activity*.

This text is concerned with these last two situations in which clusters emerge, normally of small establishments corresponding to the type of local socioterritory called *neighborhood communities*.

Thus, what we find is a historical rationale in the founding of the community. On this is imposed a political rationale constituted by space as an abstraction of place in terms of municipalities. Finally, there is the globalizing rationale with its contradictory effects: on the one hand, it is the extreme form of spatial abstraction in terms of no-places; and on the other, it revitalizes the local.

A few additional observations need to be mentioned. First, this revitalization does not mean a simple recovering of a historical place. In other more general terms, what happens is a modern recuperation of tradition, not its simple prolongation in time. Second, these rationales interact among themselves in differing ways, giving way to the identification with or opposition to territorial projects. Thus, a historic territory can be recognized on a political-administrative scale as well as revitalized by globalization. This would be the situation of maximum coincidence and could lead to a strongly developed territory. At the other extreme there could be cases where the historic project is questioned by the political-administrative configuration and in addition globalization redefines this opposition. Between these two poles fall a series of situations that tend to be more common. This

Table 1.1. Possible Community Insertions in Globalization

Resource/Mode	Exogenous	Endogenous
Labor force	Enclave	Transnational migration
Entrepreneurship	Subcontracting	Local activity

interaction of projects and the uncertainty of the concrete territory imply a third observation: the territory should be understood as a field for social action. In other words, when we speak of territorial rationales, these only exist in that social actors assume them.

SCENARIOS OF GLOBALIZATION AND
COMMUNITY INSERTIONS IN CENTRAL AMERICA

It can be said that Central America finds itself historically facing a new modernizing period. The first period corresponds to the agroexport diversification of the 1950s when cotton, sugarcane, and beef complemented the two products that had been the economic life of the region for the first half of the twentieth century: coffee and bananas. The regional industrialization through import substitution brought about a second modernization in the 1960s, which, since it did not affect the interests of the agroexport oligarchies, has been considered a hybrid of the primary export model present in Central America since the nineteenth century (Bulmer-Thomas 1989). The modernizing dynamic, induced by these two periods, came up against clear limits in the 1970s but with the crisis of the 1980s, contrary to other latitudes in Latin America, had a clearly political mark. In fact, two processes converged: first, the oligarchic crisis that had not been resolved by previous modernization attempts became evident; and second, the capitalist crisis was let loose by popular struggles in response to state authoritarianism (Torres Rivas 1987).

Two events suggest that we can speak of a new modernizing period. First, in political terms, the civil wars have been resolved, and governments have been competitively elected in all of the countries. Second, throughout the region, structural adjustment programs have been applied as a prerequisite for insertion in the globalizing process. This has meant that the state becomes the articulating axis of economic transformation subjected to opposing tendencies: the requirements of globalization (reduced state apparatus, trustworthy, financially balanced, etc.) and the demands for national integration (equity, citizen participation, etc.) (Sojo 1999). In this sense, we can say that a new modernizing period has been inaugurated in the region, characterized by three phenomena.

- We can finally say that political modernization is taking place, as expressed in the already mentioned generalized presence of democratic regimes that imply having overcome the historic pattern of oligarchic domination.
- There is a new economic attempt at modernization, but unlike the two previous ones, it does not fit within the primary export model.

As in other parts of Latin America, a new economic model is emerging with the following basic characteristics: replacement of state centrality by that of the market, trade liberalization, labor reforms and deregulation, privatization of state enterprises, and reorientation of growth from within to without (Bulmer-Thomas 1997).

- Social deficits remain, thereby making these issues the large pending debt of modernization in Central America (Pérez Sáinz 1999b).

In general terms, it can be argued that Central America is entering, as is the rest of Latin America, into a new modernity where the state is no longer the central actor and the building of the nation no longer represents the ends of the modernizing project (Robinson 1997). Rather, the market has emerged as the central instance marked by the globalizing dynamic and economic actors, firms and consumers, are those that appear to be key. In other words, the region is moving from a national modernization to a global one.

The outward reorientation of growth in Central America is fundamentally expressed in the development of three activities: new agroexports, the new assembly or *maquila* industry, and tourism. These activities constitute the principal scenarios of globalization along with another that emerges from society itself and comprises one of the main insertions of the region in this process: international labor migration. We review each one of these scenarios, outlining its dynamic and some of its basic traits, as well as the potential of community insertion in each.

Since the middle of the 1980s, an important expansion took place in what have been called *nontraditional agricultural exports*.[18] Two countries, Guatemala and Costa Rica, have mainly contributed to this expansion; in Honduras, the growth was small, and in El Salvador and Nicaragua, there was a decline in this type of export at the end of the 1980s. Its relative weight compared to all exports varies from 10 percent and 9 percent in Costa Rica and Guatemala, respectively, to 2 percent in El Salvador and Nicaragua, placing Honduras in between (6 percent). There are national differences in the composition of products. In Costa Rica, the most important has been ornamental plants (flowers, foliage, and other plants), representing 38 percent of such exports. In Guatemala, vegetables (broccoli and snow peas) constitute a fifth of this production. And in Honduras, fruit represent half of this type of export (Weller 1993).

In terms of the structure of ownership, 25 percent is controlled by transnational businesses, and 40 percent is in the hands of medium and large firms. The remaining 35 percent corresponds to smallholdings of peasant owners (Kaimowitz 1992). This means that there is a process of accumulation available for peasants, insinuating the possibility for the integration of community dynamics in this scenario.

In terms of labor, the evidence from a comparative study between Costa Rica and Honduras shows the following. First, in the case of Costa Rica, this type of activity has cushioned the job losses in agriculture that resulted from the effects of structural adjustment, while in Honduras employment generation has exceeded that lost through structural adjustment. Second, indirect employment has been generated, varying from five per direct job in Costa Rica to fourteen in Honduras. Third, these types of crops have reinforced tendencies toward salaried rural employment, with a predominance of permanent jobs in Costa Rica and temporary in Honduras. And opportunities for women have been detected that tend to pay better than other agrarian activities (Weller 1992). More focused studies have shown that female participation is key (Dary Fuentes 1991; Rojas and San Román 1993).

However, this general overview must take into account the type of crop. There are differences between groups of modern crops (such as melon or squash) compared with other, less modern ones (such as sesame seeds, Indian reed, or yucca). The first group requires more capital investment, imported technological packages, and a close integration in the stages of production, processing, and commercialization. It is also characterized by a higher use of labor and more income for the producers (Weller 1993). This productive differentiation tends to coincide with social distinctions in the sense that smaller producers concentrate fundamentally on the type of crops considered to be less modern. Regardless, the incidence of this in the peasantry should not be underestimated. In Guatemala, Baumeister (1991) has argued that there is a redefinition of the dualist model (large export-oriented farms using temporary labor and small farms to cover the cost of the peasantry in their nonproletarian periods) that represents a backbone of agricultural development in the region. The diversification toward nontraditional products, along with other factors (improved techniques, the development of nonrural activities, and emigration), has brought about a more autonomous peasantry.

Thus, there is a path for the peasantry in this scenario that could lead to a more inclusive[19] type of development and that offers possibilities for the insertion of community dynamics whose participation would not be reduced to the mere proletarianization of the labor force.

The origins of the new industrialization must be traced back to the 1970s, when attempts were made throughout all of Central America to develop new exports as a response to the regional crisis based on import substitution industrialization. Thus, during the decade, free trade zones were created in almost all the countries,[20] but for various reasons (lack of vigor in state action, the start of civil conflict, change of regime in the case of Nicaragua with the triumph of the Sandinista revolution, etc.), this experience was limited and did not allow for a new industrial pattern to emerge. It was not until the end of the 1980s, with a finalization of the economic as well as political crisis in sight, and with the generalized application of structural adjustment programs, that a new push was made for this type of industry. It has become one of the fundamental underpinnings of the new accumulative model in Central America. This thrust has translated into a proliferation of firms with the subsequent generation of employment.

The most recent estimates, and rather prudent ones, point to the creation of a quarter of a million direct jobs in the region, where the most relevant cases are Guatemala (sixty-one thousand), El Salvador (thirty-eight thousand); Honduras (seventy-five thousand), and Costa Rica (forty-eight thousand).[21] The relative weight of this new industrialization, with respect to total industrial employment, varies from 23 percent in Nicaragua to 38 percent in Guatemala (Organización International del Trabajo [OIT] 1997, 10). Diverse studies on the maquila in Central America show a common profile among the employed labor force (Pérez Sáinz and Castellanos de Ponciano 1991; Altenburg 1993; Price Waterhouse 1993; Pérez Sáinz 1994). Those employed are predominantly young people and women with relatively low levels of schooling.[22] With less security it can be said that these workers are not generally the heads of households and do not contribute the majority of their earnings to the family unit.[23]

This labor profile insinuates that the type of industry developed in the region is assembly with an intensive use of labor. In fact, the predominant industry is in apparel. However, it is not the only activity in the region, and in Costa Rica, where labor costs are higher, a diversification has taken place with the installation of high-technology businesses, especially in the field of electronics, using a more skilled labor force with less-precarious jobs. In fact, in 2000, forty-three firms with this level of technology had been detected, generating a little more than twelve thousand positions (Banco Central de Costa Rica 2001). The most notorious case is Intel, the world semiconductor leader; it initially invested $300 million, generating 2,300 positions by the end of 1998, which should grow to 3,000 when the plant development is completed with an additional $200 million of investment.[24] But prior to this, other foreign businesses in the electronics sector were already present, in addition to 130 businesses, the majority of which are Costa Rican, that develop software (Instituto Centroamericano de Administración de Empresas [INCAE]/Harvard Institute of International Development [HIID] 1999, 44).[25]

But the maquila industry has also allowed small producers to insert into global production. This insertion is mediated through subcontracting and responds to the imperatives of flexible production imposed by globalization. What is known about subcontracting by maquila firms is very limited since there are few studies concerning the topic.[26] What is interesting in these examples is that they refer to nonurban areas and therefore show that community spaces are also present in this scenario. Women are working in their homes on subcontracts, resulting from the externalization of a phase of the work process for an industrial export factory and also reflecting a hidden process of wage work. It is important to highlight two phenomena. First, the business makes functional the role of women with children who are also in the labor force, combining their reproductive and family cycles; in other words, due to household duties (fundamentally, child care), it is hard to work outside the home. Second, this type of subcontracting is extremely vertical and hierarchical, with precarious labor conditions that do not allow for possibilities for growth as self-employed workers.

The other situation corresponds to a territorial productive cluster where three issues are important.[27] Within the cluster heterogeneity can be found with different types of production arrangements in terms of subcontracting.[28] In addition, the sociocultural environment (this is an indigenous community) has involved the use of certain types of community capital. Finally, the existence in certain cases of subcontracting linkages that are less vertical has allowed for the growth of some of the establishments to the point of becoming true businesses, and thus they obtain an insertion less mediated by the globalization process.

Tourism, the third scenario, is one of the main expressions of how Central America has inserted into the current globalizing dynamics. In 1990, 1,531,634 tourists entered the region, a flow that increased to approximately a million more (2,435,115) seven years later. At the beginning of the previous decade, this activity generated $520,100,000 in income and in 1997 increased to $1,335,100,000. Two countries stand out: Guatemala and Costa Rica. But while in the first case, at the beginning of the 1990s, there were a little more than half a million tourists (508,514), more than in Costa Rica (435,037), by 1997, Costa Rica had reached 811,490 visitors, overtaking Guatemala (576,362) (Camara Nacional de Turismo [CANATUR] 1998).[29]

This is perhaps the most obvious insertion of community spaces. But this insertion can be overly subordinated if the tourist activity is organized around one hotel or several large hotels, transforming the respective community economy by integrating into globalization fundamentally through the provision of labor. But there are also cases where this activity is structured in terms of small, locally anchored establishments.[30] Just as tourism has provided a space for global insertion, some handicraft communities, given the demand for their products by tourists, have also been able to integrate into this process. Various studies in the region on some of these communities[31] demonstrate a range of elements that deserve explanation.

The origins of these handicraft activities in their respective locales are very diverse, from precolonial traditions to the nonlocal introduction of a design barely several decades old. Nonetheless, tourism, as well as the possibility to export through alternative networks of fair trade, has made dynamic the production of these handicraft communities, inserting them into globalization. These clusters of workshops present a series of rather common economic traits. First, there is not a great deal of division of labor among them that would allow for external economies of specialization. Second, the current level of technology is rather traditional. Third, the labor processes are organized in a pre-Taylorist fashion in which they are spaces for the transfer of knowledge about the trade; they thus serve as authentic schools for learning, allowing workers to become independent and set up their own establishments. Fourth, commercialization processes are diverse, varying from direct sales to the final consumer to intermediation without any further idea of the process of commercialization. Fifth, these clusters are heterogeneous, reflecting differing types of productive and commercial arrangements involving diverse types of handicraft subjects. Finally, something fundamental in terms of the economic dynamic: within the cluster, competition based on imitation prevails over that involving innovation.

These three scenarios respond to the globalization impact, through the mediated effects of structural adjustment and the presence of foreign investment in Central America. But there have also been responses from society itself. In this regard, the most important response has been without a doubt international labor migration.[32]

Three types of situations can be identified in the region. The first is emigration to the North, especially to the United States. This phenomenon affects almost all the countries of the region, but the Salvadoran case stands out. The second is the special situation of Guatemala, concretely its border with Mexico as a transit territory for the migration flow to the North. Not only are Central American migrants present in this flow but also South American, especially from the Andean countries. And the third situation refers to flows within the region. The most notorious case is that of Nicaraguans to Costa Rica (Del Cid 1992).

Because much of the flow is undocumented, we can only have a rough idea of its magnitude. The 2000 census in the United States documents 1.7 million Central Americans; 655,000 Salvadorans and 372,000 Guatemalans make up the largest two groups (Guzmán 2001). This population is neither the poorest nor the richest in their respective societies; additionally, the average educational attainment is somewhat higher than that of the respective nonmigrant nationals (Mahler 2000). Another dimension that speaks to the importance of the migration phenomenon concerns remittances. Compared with the value of exports in 1992, remittances represented 114.9 percent of the value of all exports in El Salvador and 12.6 percent, 7.1 percent, and 4.2 percent in Guatemala, Honduras, and Nicaragua, respectively (Comisión

Económica para América Latina [CEPAL] 2000, table 1.3). By 1997, remittances represented between a high of 101.6 percent (for El Salvador) and low of 20.2 percent (for Nicaragua) of the commercial deficit, with Guatemala (38.4 percent) and Honduras (58.0 percent) in intermediate positions (CEPAL 2000, table 1.3). In other words, remittances are an important source of income for the countries of the region.

In terms of migration northward, as has already been mentioned, El Salvador is the country with the highest incidence. It is estimated that approximately 15 percent of the population of this country had migrated in the 1980s, a phenomenon that has continued in the postconflict period. This labor force is characterized as being mostly male, between eighteen and twenty-five years of age, and more highly educated than the national population (Funkhouser 1992a; Andrade-Eekhoff 2002). However, it is important to point out that there is an important participation of women and that in the 1990s, more people from rural areas have been seeking opportunities in the United States (Andrade-Eekhoff 2002). Thus, migration has not just been a simple effect of the war in the 1980s. The economic transformation that has taken place in this country has meant a sharp drop in agricultural employment, some job opportunities predominantly for young women in maquila production, or openings in the financial sector for higher-skilled workers (Funkhouser and Pérez Sáinz 1998; Rivera Campos 2000). In other words, employment opportunities among certain segments of the population have been very limited.

In the Nicaraguan case, the migrant population is of working age, with higher scholastic levels and nonmanual labor background (Funkhouser 1992b). The Nicaraguan case is of particular importance since the labor market of this country has suffered the greatest changes due to the application of structural adjustment policies, measures that have principally meant the dismantling of the mixed economy developed during the Sandinista regime. Thus, there was a drastic drop in public employment, and the informal sector appears to have reached its structural limits for absorption of the labor surplus. The labor market has adjusted mainly through a spectacular increase in open unemployment.

The second mechanism has been migration to Costa Rica, which acts as a true safety valve (Funkhouser and Pérez Sáinz 1998). The labor changes in Costa Rica have favored the incorporation of Nicaraguan migrants who are employed in low-skilled jobs requiring a young labor force able to work hard. In addition to providing cheap labor, it appears that the main difference from Costa Rican workers is in terms of labor rights (Morales and Castro 1999).[33]

Obviously the migration phenomenon has many diverse impacts, which gain in importance for individuals as well as their households in terms of evaluating labor market insertion. But this insertion is embedded in social relationships, and thus it is important to talk of the social networks that encompass multiple territories. It is in this sense that migration creates links between the global and the local since the exodus of people has not meant a rupture with their place of origin. There are multiple studies in Latin and Central America that have demonstrated the diverse levels of networks and forms of exchange.[34]

Regarding this, the main level is at the household, with an emphasis on economic exchanges. Labor leaves the household, entering another locale and sending back remittances that support the family economy in the place of origin. The destiny of the migration is not random but based on familial and community relationships of those who have previously migrated. People from specific locales migrate to specific cities and obtain employment where family or friends have some sort of link. In the Salvadoran case, people from the municipality of Ozatlan, Usulutan, have sought opportunities in Houston, Texas, while the residents of Santa Elena, another nearby municipality in the same department, migrate to Los Angeles (Andrade-Eekhoff 2001). The Kanjobal of Santa Eulalia in Huehuetenango in Guatemala can be found principally in Los Angeles (Popkin 1999) due to the ties with other family members and friends who established the first migratory routes. Studies on the Nicaraguan migration to Costa Rica also point out the importance of these networks (Morales 2000).

The exchanges between the local and the global that come from international migration generate not only economic transformation but social and political ones as well. In the end, it is not just people who leave and dollars that return, and it is important to understand the complex dynamics in diverse social fields that are transnationalized through international migration.[35]

Economic exchanges are clearly the most easily perceived. The migrant leaves and sends home dollars, the fruit of his or her insertion into the labor market of another country. But this insertion produces other globalized interactions that impact the family. While many migrants leave and send home dollars and other goods, they also maintain additional ties with their families (Popkin 1999; Landolt 2001; Levitt 2001b). These ties are less tangible, and the flows can be quite irregular. However, there are diverse types of exchanges that take place and are sometimes denominated social and political remittances.

Social exchanges are carried out, impacting in the identity of the migrant as well as those family members who do not migrate. Social norms and values of what it means to be Salvadoran, Nicaraguan, or Kanjobal and from a certain family are shared and transformed between those that are here and there. These are dynamic processes where relationships and the spaces of transformation are not necessarily harmonious. For example, generational differences can be heightened when combining Americanized Kanjobal identities (Popkin 1999). Conjugal relationships can also be dramatically affected.

In terms of political exchanges in the transnationalized space of the household, in the first place citizenship issues come to the fore. Once the migrant has secured new legal rights in the receiving country, exchanges in the political arena are generated among household members. Family members in El Salvador try to stay on top of changes in U.S. migration law, concerned about the implications for their daughter, husband, or father. Upon obtaining a more permanent legal status, the migrant opens the doors of possibility for other close relatives to migrate with legal documentation. Children born in another country are members of families in a "home" country that they may never have visited but with which there exists a relationship of exchange. Living in a different society little by little introduces changes in how citizenship is lived and understood, and one way or another, this is filtered to the family who has remained in the place of origin. In synthesis, the political culture is transformed between Salvadorans, Guatemalans, or Nicaraguans living in transnationalized spaces of the household, be this in Washington, D.C., Santa Eulalia in Huehuetenango, or San José, Costa Rica (Popkin 1999; Zilberg and Lungo 1999; Morales 2000).

But exchanges from international migration do not remain exclusively in the household. To the extent that more and more people from a given locale become inserted into migration, taking advantage of the transnationalized social networks, community relationships are also transformed. In terms of economic aspects, local labor leaves to work in foreign labor markets. Depending on who leaves and who stays behind, the local labor market can be affected. Family remittances spent locally in diverse ways, and the migration process itself, can generate new economic opportunities[36] (Morales 2000; Landolt 2001). In addition to the multiplier effects of family remittances, new transnational institutions and actors send "collective remittances." These are generally used for collective or community benefit, and examples abound in the region with recreational or educational infrastructure projects, scholarships, school supplies, medical equipment, charity, and others (Andrade-Eekhoff 1997; CEPAL 2000; Orozco 2000).

These transnational actors also play a political role, forming new organizations that put pressure on local authorities and leaders. Their protagonism can be reinforced as candidates for municipal offices solicit campaign funds from these new migrant groups or when mayors travel to Los Angeles to actively promote the formation of a migration association. These migrant citizens are sometimes able to exercise more political muscle and pressure as absent residents than the actual inhabitants of the locale. Their organizing style and citizen participation can include a dose of Salvadoran political culture along with North American (Andrade-Eekhoff 1997; Landolt et. al. 1999; Landolt 2001).

At the same time, international migration generates community social changes focused on transnational/local identities. In Guatemala, the municipality of San Pedro Soloma in Huehuetenango welcomes visitors to the town with a sign proudly displayed at the entrance in Spanish, Kanjobal, and English. In Intipuca in eastern El Salvador, the streets are called Washington, Jefferson, and Walker, in reference to former presidents of the United States and a former U.S. ambassador to the country. Obviously the transformations of community identity go well beyond these superficial examples. But they demonstrate a reference point to an "other" that is located in a transnationalized community space where the reference is the community of migrants in Los Angeles or Washington, D.C., whose identities develop around those people who are closest to their daily life. In the case of Central Americans in the United States, this is a very diverse population including African Americans, Chicanos, and Koreans (Zilberg 1997). The study of the Kanjobal migrant community of Santa Eulalia, Huehuetenango, also points to the emergence of a transnational identity that has recouped old forms of ethnicity through the household, community institutions, and religious organizations in particular (Popkin 1999).

Global transformations in Central American societies, and in particular the Salvadoran, are probably greater due to international migration. Entering into globalization from "below" by exporting labor is generating changes not only among households but also at a community level. It is in this sense that international labor migration opens a wide door to globalization for local communities, even if this is a back door.

Thus, each of these scenarios demonstrates community spaces that can be inserted into globalizing dynamics. The problem is that this insertion is not very visible, and globalization tends to be perceived through more prominent actors: large business, especially transnational. As we have argued in the introduction, one of the principal objectives of this study is to make visible these local community actors diffused by the dazzling images of "official" globalization. This task we take up in the next chapter.

NOTES

1. In this separation, the primacy of time over space has been emphasized, which has led to the production of images that distance society from the material environment. This is the well-known distinction of the Enlightenment discourses between "culture" and "nature," with their aftereffects in terms of the construction of "masculine" and "feminine" (Coronil 2000).

2. But the construction of the absent figure has generated a serious cultural problem for Western rationalism: death. This absence has intrinsic difficulties for rationalization because of its definitive and total nature. However, premodern cultures have the advantage that, having not constructed the figure of absence, the dead continue to be present in different ways.

3. This reinterpretation is not alien to that of Giddens that pointed to money as one of the principal means of distancing space from time.

4. McGrew (1992) has identified three major foci concerning global politics. He considers the *realist* approach in terms of cooperation and conflict between nation-states where their power is the key variable. The *liberal-pluralist*, on the contrary, sees the existence of a global system based on polyarchy. Finally, the *neo-Marxist* emphasizes the accented control of capital over the globalized scene.

5. The other reason has to do with the battle for the imagination that is being waged between the two in a cannibalistic fashion.

6. This view basically argues that current changes reflect only a highly internationalized economy but have not led to any radical transformation of capitalism. The opposite view would be that of the hyperglobalizer that, on the contrary, posits that today only globalized markets and transnational firms count and that neither can be governed by national states (Ohmae 1990, 1995). For a critique of both views revindicating an intermediary position, see Perraton et al. (1997) and Held et al. (1999).

7. This type of argument can be taken to the extreme leading to the transterritorialization of the nation-state as posited by the view denominated "transnationalism from below" (as opposed to that from above, fruit of capital and its institutions) (Guarnizo and Smith 1998). For a balanced view of the problems and potential of this field of study, see Mahler (1998).

8. This phenomenon of the Fordist model was the object of reflection during the 1970s and 1980s in regulationist schools. These theories were framed within the reinterpretations that took place concerning the development of capitalism after the 1970s. Jessop (1990) has identified seven differing schools of regulation.

9. There were two additional elements. First, an intensive regime of accumulation dominated where productivity development was reached thanks to the more efficient use of inputs required for production, especially in the labor force. The production of relative surplus value was prioritized. Second, the foundation for this process materialized through the Fordist industrial model called *Fordist*. In this model, Taylorist organizational principles (the separation of conception activities from those of execution, resulting in the simplification of the latter) were incorporated into the semiautomatic assembly line (Dundford 1990).

10. This idea of disorder can be assimilated with the concept of a society of risk postulated by Beck (1998). He argues that we have moved from an industrial society, where risks were limited to groups and places, to a new situation where global threats (his own terminology) affect everyone and do not respect national borders.

11. One answer to this contradiction, according to Swyngedouw (1992), is the configuration of what is called the "hollow corporation" that maintains control of technological activities, design, finance, and marketing while relocating those

of production. This is an intensive firm in the first set of activities and extensive in the second.

12. Amin (1994) has pressed this thesis, arguing that, due to this contradiction, there should be a return to structures of a national nature to regulate capital.

13. We wish to point out that from here on we will use the terms *local, place,* and *locale* indifferently.

14. In their appendix on examples of globalized urban nodes, Borja and Castells (1997) include São Paulo. But what their text shows is only a deep sociospatial inequality as the characteristic of this city.

15. This type of community differs from that of blood, sustained through the family and kinship, as well as that of the spiritual, based on friendship and religious in nature and located in the city, as was proposed by Tonnies. The adjective *neighborhood* also highlights that this type of community is fixed territorially. In principle, as Ayora Díaz (2000) argues well, a community has no spatial limits but depends on the imagination of its members.

16. Obviously, there is also the other side of the coin: the marginalization of local territory as a product of the exclusionary effects of globalizing dynamics.

17. Entrepreneurship should be understood laxly as an initiative of self-employment oriented toward accumulation rather than subsistence.

18. This term is understood in the literature to be all agricultural exports, new or otherwise, except for coffee, bananas, cotton, and sugarcane.

19. The Guatemalan case (concretely the production of winter vegetables) has been interpreted in these terms due to the increased access to land and the generation of employment (Carter, Barham, and Mesbah 1996).

20. Costa Rica is the exception, but a regime of tariff privileges for export assembly industries was implemented. These businesses were located in the metropolitan zone of the Central Valley.

21. In Nicaragua, the impact is much less because this process is rather new.

22. However, given the low levels of education in the region, with the exception of Costa Rica, maquila laborers cannot be considered to be poorly educated (Comisión Económica para América Latina [CEPAL] 1994).

23. Nonetheless, in a study of maquila workers in Guatemala City, two groups of women were clearly identified: young with few family responsibilities and older, generally single, heads of households subjected to a double day of work (factory and household) (Pérez Sáinz and Castellanos de Ponciano 1991).

24. For an analysis of this firm and the chains that it has induced in Costa Rica, see Spar (1998) and Hershberg and Monge (2000).

25. This type of development is still very new in the rest of the region even though technical advice services exist in El Salvador for foreign electronics equipment using international telephone companies. There is also the presence of a few foreign firms of electronic assembly in Honduras, and a certain amount of development of software and data processors in Guatemala.

26. The first was carried out by Pérez Sáinz and Leal (1992) in San Pedro Sacatepéquez, Guatemala, one of the three case studies included in this text, and will therefore be analyzed in greater detail in the coming chapters. There are also several studies on subcontracted home work in rural communities in the Sula Valley of Honduras (Pérez Sáinz 1999b)

27. This is the case of San Pedro Sacatepéquez. What is mentioned here refers to the main findings from the first study on this community.

28. With regard to this point, it also needs to be mentioned that in this cluster clothing design and production existed prior to the generalization of maquila subcontracting.

29. In the Costa Rican case, these numbers must be used with caution since Nicaraguan visitors have been included, and they generally come to Costa Rica as migrant laborers and not as tourists.

30. The case study on tourism included in this work corresponds precisely to this situation. But there are also studies in Flores, Guatemala (Cordero 2000), and Quepos in Costa Rica (Van der Duim et al. 2001).

31. These studies refer to the case of Sarchí in Costa Rica (Pérez Sáinz and Cordero 1994), various Salvadoran communities (Pérez Sáinz and Andrade-Eekhoff 1998), and Comalapa in Guatemala (Pérez Sáinz 1999a). We should mention that one of the Salvadoran communities is La Palma, one of the universes that will be explored in greater detail in the coming chapters.

32. It must be pointed out that the civil wars in the region also generated large displacements of population within the countries, in the region, and toward Mexico.

33. Additionally, one must remember that some migrations take place in border areas. The most complete study on this matter is that of Morales (1996). It is also important to mention the significant level of temporary migration of Guatemalan agricultural workers to Chiapas, Mexico (Castillo 1990).

34. See in particular the special edition of *Ethnic and Racial Studies,* volume 2 (March 1999), dedicated to the topic of transnational communities; and *Global Networks: A Journal of Transnational Affairs,* volume 1, number 3 (July 2001), in which migrant transnationalism is theorized through recent research projects.

35. A series of articles published recently link migration with transnationalization, a concept that has generally been used in referring to the global activities of large businesses. For more analytical perspectives on the use of the term *transnational* and its link to migration, see in particular Portes, Guarnizo, and Landolt (1999); Levitt (2001a); and Portes (2001).

36. For example, local informal parcel carriers known as *encomenderos* travel between the community of origin and the places where migrants live, carrying packages to and from migrants and their families; Central American products are exported to be consumed in what has come to be called the "nostalgic market"; and, of course, there is the example of the economic activities of *coyotes,* who charge considerable sums to escort undocumented people to the North.

2

Locale and
Social Dynamics

As we mentioned in the introduction, we offer a view of local dynamics from the perspective of social (dis)integration. Our thesis is that the viability and sustainability of an insertion in the process of globalization ultimately depends on the cohesion of the locale as a community. Thus, the point of departure should be an understanding of the dynamics that affect local social (dis)integration. By adopting this interpretative perspective, we privilege the household as our analytical unit since it constitutes the main social space where reproduction of the members in the community materializes. Obviously this reproduction implies multiple dimensions, material as well as symbolic. In this chapter, we will limit ourselves to the material reproduction of households, trying to identify the factors that affect this. This exercise will set the stage for the analytical approach concerning the economic activity that allows the respective locale to be inserted in the globalization process as well the existing political-institutional configuration, which is part of the next chapter. In other words, we will interpret the question of insertion in globalization from a social perspective. This is our methodological proposal.

Following the interpretive route, in this chapter we wish to describe the households in each of the three locales, given that the domestic unit is the analytical reference point, par excellence: this description will be complemented with an analysis of the levels of social (dis)integration found in each community. This sets the foundation for moving onto a multivariate exercise, in the same section, that identifies the various factors associated with the material welfare of the household. The multidimensional analysis will permit the first overall view of the local dynamics needed to delve into the respective labor markets since income generated in these is crucial in determining the effects of social (dis)integration. In this regard, we consider that these are fields for social action by individual domestic units. This task will be taken up in the following section, identifying the rationale of labor insertion used by households. In this way, the overall view will be enriched in a final section analyzing the expressions of differing rationales (traditional, modern, and global) that configure the socioterritoriality, as argued in the previous chapter. Questions for discussion will be introduced so that they may be addressed in the next chapter. But to begin this task, we need to describe the three locales that make up our empirical points of references for the reflections in this as well as the other chapters.

THE UNIVERSES OF STUDY

Our cases are three Central American communities that, through different routes, have formed clusters of small business linked to an activity inserted in the globalizing dynamics affecting the region. These communities are (1) La Fortuna in Costa Rica, linked with tourism; (2) La Palma in El Salvador, the main handicraft community of the country; and (3) San Pedro Sacatepéquez in Guatemala, a community invigorated by export manufacturing subcontracting, specifically in apparel. In this section we will limit ourselves to summarizing the historical process of formation of these territories, emphasizing the formation of the respective clusters and how they have been inserted into globalization.

The case that refers to tourism, La Fortuna, is the seventh district of the *cantón*[1] of San Carlos in the province of Alajuela in Costa Rica. It is 225 square kilometers and in 1999 had a population of approximately 7,500. This locale is reached easily since there is a highway in good condition that links it with the district of Ciudad Quesada, seat of the cantón, and another connecting to San Ramón. A concentration of services from supermarkets to banks can be found in the center. There is also a health clinic, a public school, and a technical professional school.

La Fortuna has traditionally been an agricultural area growing tubers and roots, raising cattle, and engaging in agroindustry. The Yucca Fair that used to be held in this town was well known and offered visitors a wide variety of products derived from this vegetable. But once the Arenal volcano erupted in 1968, tourism increased in La Fortuna. The attraction of the active and conic-shaped volcano led a large number of foreigners to visit the area. With the Costa Rican boom in tourism in the mid-1980s, tourism to La Fortuna increased substantially. Local informants coincide in pointing out that "everyone who came to Costa Rica also came here to La Fortuna. No one wants to leave without having seen el Arenal erupting lava."

In 1990, this town had only two hotels and a few cabins used mostly for national tourism; toward the end of the decade, there were more than fifty establishments[2] for lodging and more than a dozen for eating. Other evidence of growth in tourism in the area can be found in the number of beds available: in 1992, there was a capacity of 90 beds; and by the end of the 1990s, there were more than 1,700. It is important to mention that one of the fundamental characteristics that differentiates the development of tourism in this locale is the predominance of small enterprises owned by people from La Fortuna. There are 125 tourist businesses of all sorts in La Fortuna, of which 120 are in the hands of people who grew up in the region. These businesses cover a wide variety of tourist services: lodging, restaurants, excursions, bicycle rentals and horseback riding, souvenir shops, and so forth. At the same time, the area of La Fortuna offers a wide variety of recreational opportunities for tourists; in addition to contemplating the Arenal volcano, visitors may enjoy horseback rides to Monteverde, excursions to the Caño Negro lagoon, and other activities.[3]

La Palma, the Salvadoran handicraft community, is located about eighty kilometers north of the capital, San Salvador, in the northern part of Chalatenango, on a highway known as the Northern Route, connecting with the Honduran border. This road, one of the principal border routes with the neighboring country, has been repaved but until quite recently seemed more like a rural road than an international highway, due to the poor conditions that deteriorated each day with the passing of trailer trucks and heavy winter rains. According to the most recent census data, in 1992 the municipality had a population of 10,632 inhabitants, of which a little more than a quarter lived in what is considered the urban area (Dirección General de Estadística y Censos [DIGESTYC] 1992). During the civil war in the 1980s, heavy combat between the FMLN (Farabundo Marti National Liberation Front) and the army took place in this area, displacing many people to other parts of the country or even causing them to seek refuge in Honduras. Agricultural production of corn, beans, and coffee, historically the most important crops, is made more difficult due to the orography of the area and land that is too acidic for cultivation. Some manufacturing exists in nearby San Ignacio, ten kilometers from La Palma, where toothpicks are produced. National tourism has been developing[4] but has suffered difficulties due to the poor condition of the roads.

In 1971, various people, including the now nationally famous painter Fernando Llort, arrived to live in La Palma, seeking the tranquility of the pine trees in the mountains. These young artists formed a commune, and even though their economic needs were not pressing, they sought out activities that could provide them with an income as well as take advantage of their artistic skills. They began to carve wood and then started using the *copinol* seed,[5] drawing intricate designs on both. This initiated the handicraft activity. These artists formed the first workshop, calling it *Semilla de Dios* (Seed of God), which was legally founded as a cooperative in 1977, serving as a source of work for young people who began to learn the trade and develop their own artistic skills. By the beginning of the 1980s, as a resident said, "the young people began to have problems and little by little set up their own workshops."

In this way, more and more workshops slowly formed, each adding something new to the artistic environment. While it is recognized that the handicraft activities in La Palma were born as an initiative of Fernando Llort and other artists from San Salvador, it is now considered the patrimony of La Palma. One artisan considers that "handicrafts are the patrimony of La Palma. Fernando Llort is a link in this patrimony. He set up a strategy for commercialization and a sellable product. But Fernando Llort left La Palma in 1980 [when the civil war intensified and the region came under control of the FMLN], and the crafts have evolved. Each workshop has added something to the design. There are two basic designs: Llort's geometrical design and the natural one from La Palma."

By 1980, there were already fourteen workshops, and la Semilla de Dios began to penetrate the international market. The decade, marked by civil conflict in the country and with La Palma, as already mentioned as a place of combat, paradoxically saw the growth of handicraft activities. Several factors explain this development: the return of Fernando Llort to San Salvador, where he established an art gallery that displayed and sold La Palma handicrafts, mainly to international tourists; the consolidation of the international handicrafts marketplace, the International Fair in San Salvador created in the 1970s; and the development of the project *Casa de las Artesanías*, or "House of Crafts," promoted by an NGO. Obviously, the backdrop for all this was the visibility of the country on the world scene, unfortunately due to the armed conflict.

The beginning of the 1980s was marked by price wars, considered to be unfair competition between the cooperative and other workshops, and the domination of the market by nonlocal intermediaries. As a result, an effort was made between 1984 and 1986 to unite producers with the objective of eliminating the intermediaries. Workshop owners met weekly to analyze the role of the intermediaries and seek alternatives. In 1986, the Agricultural Foment Bank (BFA) provided financing to the tune of two million *colones* to set up a commercialization project. A cooperative of producers was formed, and the bank disbursed the first payment. However, the experience was negative, and the bank cut off further economic support, ending the project. In this same period, wood began to become harder to obtain. Faced with this situation, la Semilla de Dios was the only workshop to respond proactively to the problem by purchasing a piece of land and cultivating wood for use in the handicrafts. Despite the need, no other workshops have had enough capital to make this sort of investment. Actually, one of the more critical problems facing the workshops is obtaining wood.

Paradoxically, the war was a prosperous period for handicraft production in La Palma. Between 1986 and 1990, the number of workshops grew from twenty to more than one hundred. This was its apogee, and there were workshops of many sizes (small, medium, and large) with a variety of quality and forms of production. The smallest workshops functioned mainly with family labor (especially children) and a minimal of quality and outside workers; the larger ones used a greater division of labor, with paid workers from the community. Since 1990, handicraft production and sales have dropped off. Some artisans consider that this is due to the lack of international publicity of the country and the lack of support from international aid agencies. However, there is also competition from other workshops that were set up in other towns and have trained people there. As part of the process of demobilization of the FMLN, ex-combatants with skills in handicrafts trained other ex-combatants, and some set up workshops or cooperatives in other parts of Chalatenango and even in San Salvador.

In terms of the Guatemala universe, San Pedro Sacatepéquez is the municipal seat, under the jurisdiction of the department of Guatemala, in the central area of the country. It is about twenty-five kilometers from the center of the capital but due to the growth of the metropolitan area (which ends at about kilometer eighteen) is just seven kilometers away. The community can be reached by a heavily traveled highway transited by trailers, commercial trucks, and urban and regional buses. This road is an extension of the San Juan Highway toward the northwest of the city, cutting through an industrial zone and poorer settlements. Between the end of the San Juan Highway and San Pedro Sacatepéquez are at least six large maquila factories, as well as a series of warehouses, factories (of construction materials and shoes), hardware stores, and a variety of commercial stores. The highway to the community is in good condition since this and another main city road receive regular maintenance. The asphalt road extends into San Pedro Sacatepéquez. However, the roads to other nearby municipal districts or rural communities are unpaved or in very poor condition, as in the case of San Raymundo, Chuarrancho, and Santo Domingo Xenacoj—all places with which San Pedro Sacatepéquez maintains commercial relationships and where labor is also recruited for work in the San Pedro shops.

The *Kaqchiquels*[6] referred to the place where the town of San Pedro Sacatepéquez lies as *Ucubil* due to its elevation at the foot of a high hill.

Various references to this appear in colonial chronicles from the beginning of the seventeenth century. It is believed that the municipality was founded in 1769 when neighbors to the area bought approximately 422 *caballerías* plus one *legua of ejidos*[7] from the Spanish Crown. In 1899, Chuarrancho seceded and became part of San Raimundo, later constituting a separate municipality. In 1932, San Pedro Sacatepéquez was separated from this municipality; five years later, the village Buena Vista was annexed to it. In 1909, potable water was introduced, and forty years later mail and telegraph services were established. During the 1960s, a health clinic was set up, along with electrical services, a primary school, and a high school. The main fair is celebrated during the three days of carnival, which has no set date. The municipality has a town center (divided into four zones that correspond to old annexed rural areas), three villages (Buena Vista, Chillaní, and Vista Hermosa), and nine rural districts (Gall 1983).

The most recent official census, from 1994, reports a population of 21,009 inhabitants, of which 41.7 percent reside in the urban area. Eighty-eight percent of the residents of this municipality consider themselves to be indigenous, of Kakchiquel descent. The data also reveal that half of the economically active population works in manufacturing and a fifth in commerce. Agricultural activities employ less than 10 percent of the labor force (Instituto Nacional de Estadística [INE] 1996). In fact, this activity stopped being of any importance some time ago. Initially, it was commercial activities that began to displace the ancestral activities of this town as an expression of the modernization affecting indigenous communities in Guatemala.[8] And it was precisely a merchant that unchained the manufacturing revolution in San Pedro Sacatepéquez. It is worthwhile to recover his testimony from a previous study carried out in this community, since he has since retired from economic activities but is widely recognized within the community (Pérez Sáinz and Leal 1992, 16):

I began in Guatemala [the capital] in 1958 with a pedal sewing machine. Then, seeing that it was necessary to grow I thought about coming here to San Pedro, and thinking about the future of San Pedro, well, it wasn't in my interest to stay in Guatemala. I worked for one year in the capital and then moved to here in 1960. That was when I set up the first factory here in San Pedro Sacatepéquez. Of course back then no one could work like this on a sewing machine; I had to teach each one until they learned, and I was able to establish a factory with twenty people. At that time there was no electricity, so we had to work on requesting electricity, which we were able to obtain. Then the nomenclature of San Pedro needed to be set up with zones, addresses and streets and avenues. I worked a lot on this so that San Pedro could triumph. And then when we got electricity, I thought it was no longer possible to continue working without industrial machinery. And that was how we started using industrial sewing machines here in San Pedro Sacatepéquez. And a lot of the people that worked with me, separated themselves after they had soaked up the process of making shirts and started out in their own place.

This monograph identifies various phases in the development of the activity of apparel production in San Pedro Sacatepéquez. From 1960 to 1967, the activity used rudimentary technology—specifically, pedaled sewing machines. In 1969, electricity was introduced into the town thanks to the committee organized by the person who was a pioneer in the development of this activity. In this way electric machines were acquired and used (this was one of the main reasons for establishing electrical service), and a second stage was initiated, marked by modernization of the equipment.

During this same period, the 1976 earthquake destroyed homes and places of work. In some cases, new machinery had to be purchased through loans, thus consolidating the modernization process that involved the use of specialized electrical machinery for specific functions (buttonholers, overlocks, etc.).

The third milestone was in 1987 when maquila production began to operate in a substantial manner in the country and subcontracting in San Pedro became more generalized, inaugurating the current moment of development of industrial apparel making (Pérez Sáinz and Leal 1992). Another key person for the community entered the picture at this time: Alvaro Colom. His initial contacts with the San Pedrans were through the sales of sewing machines, but later he was the representative in Guatemala of a large North American clothing manufacturer, which established the first large subcontract in San Pedro Sacatepéquez (discussed further in chapter 4).[9]

With this brief description of the genesis of these clusters and their respective insertions in globalization, we can take up the analysis of these universes and compare the underlying issues of the community dynamics.

HOUSEHOLDS AND SOCIAL INTEGRATION

To bring into context the analysis carried out in this chapter, it is important to present a description of the households in each community.[10] This is done with table 2.1. The table indicates differing profiles for each locale. In La Fortuna, two phenomena stand out. On the one hand, there is a more unfavorable labor dependency ratio but, on the other, a higher educational level of the head of household. This last fact, of greater relevance, refers back to the location of this universe, in Costa Rica where educational levels are higher than in El Salvador and Guatemala. It is probable that this is also associated with the globalized activity, tourism, requiring educational levels higher than those of the activities in the other two locales, where formal human capital is not as critical as in the Costa Rican case.

The most important trait in La Palma is, without a doubt, the high percentage of households headed by women. This could be related to the aftermath of the conflict in the 1980s (this community, as has been mentioned, was a site of armed conflict) and/or migration processes.

Finally, in San Pedro Sacatepéquez we find larger families, but they also involve more members of the household in the labor market; as can been seen, it has the lowest labor dependency ratio among the three locales. It must be remembered that the indigenous population predominates (84.8 percent of the households) and that these demographic and labor traits are typical of this ethnic group. Educational attainment among the heads of household is also the lowest, a result that is not surprising given that the community is in Guatemala and, more important, an indigenous one.

With this first approximation we can begin to identify the levels of social integration in each of the communities. This overview can be seen in table 2.2, which presents an estimation of poverty[11] levels but incorporates a new category: that of integration with risk of impoverishment.

Table 2.1.   Household Profiles by Locale

Variables	La Fortuna (n = 173)	La Palma (n = 245)	San Pedro Sacatepéquez (n = 262)	Total* (n = 680)	p <*
Number of members (average)	4.5	4.7	5.2	4.9	.009
Demographic dependency ratio[a] (average)	0.6	0.8	0.6	0.7	.002
Labor dependency ratio[b] (average)	2.6	2.4	2.1	2.3	.001
Female head of household (%)	28.0	39.5	25.7	30.9	.003
Educational level of household head (average in years)	7.1	4.5	4.0	4.9	.000

*Analysis of variance for metric variables and chi-squared for nonmetric variables.
[a]Coefficient of number of people less than twelve and more than sixty-four years of age, divided by the rest.
[b]Coefficient of household size divided by number of employed members of the household.
Source: FLACSO survey.

With this category we challenge traditional dichotomous views (impoverishment vs. nonimpoverishment) of social integration and thus emphasize the problem of vulnerability that, in contexts that are not marked by socioeconomic polarization, is of great relevance.

The most suggestive proposal concerning this point has been formulated by Minujin (1998), who offers a redefinition for understanding social (dis)integration in terms of the triad of exclusion/vulnerability/inclusion to capture the complexity of socioeconomic dynamics. This author presents various reasons concerning the pertinence of this type of focus. The first is that he redefines the question of integration in terms of citizenship, especially social, where needs are rights.[12] Second, he offers a dynamic view of (dis)integration, overcoming dichotomous and static analyses. Finally, this makes possible an integral perspective offering a general framework for a series of similar notions such as marginality and poverty.[13]

Based on these three reasons, Minujin proposes the existence of two profoundly interrelated dynamics of exclusion/inclusion: economic and social. In the first, the skill level of labor, type of employment, and level of productivity are fundamental. In the second it is the type of resources managed by the household: income, availability of different types of capital (social, cultural, etc.), and the existence of public coverage and access to important basic services. The result of this interaction, according to this set of classifying criteria, produces these three social zones: inclusion, vulnerability, and exclusion. Minujin describes the case of vulnerability, the intermediate zone that interests us: It is made up of poor sectors with possibilities for inclusion and by impoverished middle sectors; this sector has grown more in recent years and thus has its relevance as well. The two groups that make up this sector demonstrate certain types of comparative advantages (informal vs. formal culture); and while

Table 2.2. Social Integration of Households by Locale and Levels of Integration

Levels of Integration	La Fortuna (n = 173)	La Palma (n = 245)	San Pedro Sacatepéquez (n = 262)	Total* (n = 680)
Integration	56.0	48.1	37.4	45.8
Integration with risk of impoverishment	28.9	17.6	1.9	14.3
Poverty	8.7	22.9	33.2	23.3
Extreme poverty	6.4	11.4	27.5	16.6
Total	100.0	100.0	100.0	100.0

*Chi-squared *p* = .000
Source: FLACSO survey.

downward social mobility predominates, there are also individual successes leading to upward social mobility.[14]

However, in this text we have opted for an understanding of vulnerability limited to integrated households and based on the idea of risk. This concept has become central to the understanding of changes in modernity as presented by Beck (1998). Some time ago, this German sociologist warned that we were entering a new phase of modernity marked by risk. He posited the rise of a new attribute of danger similar to the destiny of certain traditional societies such as those of medieval Europe. To back up his argument, this author developed two ideas. First, the production of risk today competes with and even imposes itself on the production of wealth. In the previous industrial phase of modernity, the logic of wealth imposed a social distribution of risk. But today, productive forces have lost their innocence and risk affects the civilization as a whole. Second, Beck has developed what he calls the theorem of individualization. The development of the welfare state has meant the detraditionalization of the way of life of industrial society. The system of classes, the nuclear family with its "normal biographies," and professional trajectories have been diluted. The individual has been left free to confront risk. The main consequence of this, according to Beck, is the operation of a radical redefinition of modernization that presents itself as an issue and problem. In other words, modernity has become reflexive.[15]

Without fully adopting Beck's proposals, whose reference points are societies in the North and more specifically Beck's native land, we consider that the notion of risk is pertinent to understanding the changes that are taking place in Latin America and more concretely in Central America. In this regard, we would posit that our region is moving from what can be called a national modernization to one that can be considered global. This national modernization has been marked by the Latin American development of the previous decades in which the main objective was the constitution of the nation and whose principal actor was the state.[16] But since the crisis of the 1980s and the subsequent application of structural adjustment programs in the region, the force of this modernizing model has been seriously questioned. We currently face the emergence of a new model where it would appear that the modernizing rationale is that of the insertion of economies and societies in the globalization process with more diffuse actors (firms and consumers) defined primarily by a mercantile logic.

It is precisely the combination of the primacy of the market with its global orientation that makes the phenomenon of risk an important issue in this new modernization. What needs to be highlighted is the volatility of the markets. In the market of tradable goods so crucial to the new accumulative model, consumption has been individualized, losing its indifferent character of mass and bringing to the fore its symbolic function subjected to permanent changes. The issue of volatility is even clearer in the case of financial markets, which are the most globalized and where the virtual economy has reached its greatest expression as a result of the revolution in communications. But the market where people are inserted to ensure their reproduction is also affected: the labor market. This is also a globalized market through international migratory flows where risk is one of the main factors. But this phenomenon has also penetrated national labor markets through its deregulation and the resulting precariousness. The risky nature of labor dynamics greatly affects social integration, generating vulnerability.

In this regard, it is important to identify the causes that generate this risk. In terms of the poverty-line methodology, risk is manifested through the deterioration of household income. There are two sources for this risk. The first is inflation, which affects all types of income, whether from labor or other. This risk can be neutralized, to varying degrees, by the rate of exchange if there is foreign income. In this regard, one can consider savings accounts in dollars, a phenomenon that is relatively common among the Latin American middle class (potential candidates for the risk zone) or migrant remittances, which are playing an important role in some cases in poverty reduction.[17] Additionally, inflation can also be neutralized by active salary policies.[18] This was probably the most important cause of risk during the 1980s, especially in those countries that faced hyperinflationary processes. The second source of risk is the loss of employment and is more relevant today given the labor effects of the new mode of accumulation. For this reason, as well as for analytical simplicity, our interpretation is limited to this second cause of risk.

Concretely, the risk of impoverishment[19] has been estimated as the possibility of integrated households falling below the poverty line if their incomes were reduced, based on the probability of unemployment. It is important to mention that this probability is understood in a broad manner as not simply being limited to the rate of open unemployment but rather taking into account discouraged unemployment (people considered to be inactive from a labor market point of view, but willing to work) and visible underemployment equivalent to partial involuntary unemployment. Each one of these components reflects relevant issues. In regard to open unemployment, the rates throughout the 1990s in Latin America have been the same as they were in the mid-1980s at the height of the external debt crisis. In other words, the new accumulative model includes structural unemployment as one of its inherent characteristics, constituting at the same time one of the most novel traits in the reconfiguration of labor markets. Discouraged unemployment permits a diachronic view of unemployment, allowing for a better understanding of the same. And visible underemployment refers to the problem of part-time work that, under the new labor conditions, may be emerging as an increasingly relevant phenomenon (Pérez Sáinz and Mora Salas 2001).

Returning to table 2.2, we may draw two basic conclusions. First, the differences in the levels of impoverishment, and within these the rates of extreme poverty, reflect national differences. Historically, Costa Rica has stood out from the rest of Central America for its lower poverty rates. However, during the 1990s, El Salvador experienced a respectable reduction in poverty. As we have already mentioned in note 17 in this chapter, this reduction can be explained by the massive influx of remittances confirming that this is the principal means of global insertion for this country. These national differences are reproduced in our universes but at a smaller scale, suggesting that these are contexts with higher levels of welfare than the national averages of each respective country.

The second conclusion is that we see an opposing relationship between poverty and the risk of impoverishment since as poverty increases, the risk of falling into poverty is lower and vice versa. In other words, this phenomenon is irrelevant in situations of socioeconomic polarization. On the other hand, overcoming poverty does not mean that vulnerability has disappeared but quite the contrary. This means that the social mobility barrier is not limited to the poverty line but rather there is a barrier which is less perceptible, but perhaps more impenetrable—the risk of impoverishment. This analysis demonstrates that it cannot be forgotten that in the two locales where integration dominates (La Palma and mainly La Fortuna), there are respectable percentages of households at risk of falling into poverty. This presents potential consequences in the global insertion process for either consolidating social integration or increasing poverty levels.

With this analysis, we now move toward a more integrated view of the dynamics that affect each locale. We use a multivariable analysis[20] where the dependent variable is the same one that has been used in the previous paragraphs to determine the situation of (dis)integration of the households in each of the three universes under consideration: per capita income as an indicator of material welfare. We carry out this exercise for each locale to compare them and thus determine which factors have universal applicability versus those that emphasize the particularities of each universe of study. In this sense, it is pertinent to justify the analytical dimensions that we have selected.

We take into account the demographic composition of the household, highlighting its importance as the analytical unit in this exercise. The considerations concerning the household unit are complemented with the incorporation of the importance of the level of female headship among the households as an expression of sociodemographic transformations generating new family arrangements.[21] At the same time, educational levels can reveal the incidence of the state in this social field that incorporates the most basic of social policies. This is a doubly important factor: it incorporates the national dimension into the analysis and invites reflections on the type of development present in the country of the respective locale. In other words, it provides a context for the universes of study in terms of broader territories, while allowing for a diachronic look at the data.

Along with these three sociodemographic dimensions, labor factors are also fundamental since they project the analysis from the household into the respective cluster through the labor market. In this regard, we have tried to capture the different strategies used by households in terms of the distribution of their main reproductive resource, their labor force, through different options in the labor market. Here we consider the number of people working outside the local economy, particularly important in one of the cases, the Guatemalan, where the community is located near the national capital. Within the local labor market we take into account insertions in the globalized activity (tourism in La Fortuna, handicrafts in La Palma, and apparel manufacturing in San Pedro Sacatepéquez). We also consider employment in the modern as well as traditional sectors. This segmentation, whose analytical pertinence will be discussed in the next section,[22] allows (up to a certain point) diachronic comparisons[23] since the three local segments that have been identified correspond to distinct logics of community formation, as argued in the previous chapter. Obviously, their interaction with the present changes them, thus posing certain limitations in this analytical exercise. The results of the three models are presented in table 2.3, analyzed comparatively between the three locales.

Three variables have similar results in each of the universes and thus imply certain universal tendencies. These are precisely the sociodemographic variables. The demographic dependency ratio, as expected, is inversely related with per capita income. However, it is important to point out the contrast between the Costa Rican universe (the higher level of significance) with that of the Guatemalan (the lowest) since the dependency ratio is the same in both locales, as can be seen in the first table in this section. This is related to the higher level of mobilization of labor resources among Guatemalan households, as we will analyze later.[24] In other words, this mobilization tends to partly neutralize the demographic determinants demonstrating the incidence of basic sociocultural behaviors.

The new family arrangements have a respectable presence: 27.5 percent of households in La Fortuna, 39.2 percent in La Palma, and 25.1 percent in San Pedro Sacatepéquez are headed by women. However, female headship is not significantly associated with lower per capita incomes, implying that this type of household does not have a greater probability of finding itself in a situation of poverty, as is generally thought.[25] In other words, the hypothesis concerning the feminization of poverty cannot be confirmed.

Table 2.3.   Multiple Linear Regression Models of the Decimal Logarithm of Per Capita
Income with Selected Predictors by Locale

Variable	La Fortuna	La Palma	San Pedro Sacatepéquez
Demographic dependency ratio	-.184**	-.114**	-.090*
	(.042)	(.030)	(.040)
Educational level of	.033**	.021**	.017**
household head	(.006)	(.007)	(.006)
Female-headed household	.017	.031	-.010
	(.057)	(.056)	(.053)
Number of global jobs	.111**	-.026	.104**
	(.031)	(.030)	(.020)
Number of modern jobs	.047	.123*	.032
	(.038)	(.050)	(.075)
Number of traditional jobs	.064*	-.019	.034
	(.032)	(.033)	(.028)
Number of nonlocal jobs	.118	.091	.092**
	(.087)	(.073)	(.040)
Constant	4.334**	2.673**	2.306**
	(.081)	(.075)	(.064)
Adjusted R^2	.294	.150	.164
F	.000	.000	.000
N	167	204	255

*$p < .05$.
**$p < .01$.
Source: FLACSO survey.

Educational levels produce the expected results, but what is interesting are the levels of statistical significance reflecting the differing degrees of incidence of education in each of the respective countries, showing at the same time the levels of social development that have already been reached. Thus, in the Costa Rican case, this variable has the highest incidence, while at the opposite end we find the Guatemalan universe. The Salvadoran case is in between. This scale perfectly reflects the educational averages of the household head observed in table 2.1.[26]

However, the variables related to the labor insertion of the household present differing results in each of the three universes.[27] In this regard, the first thing to mention is the number of members of the household that make up the occupational structure. The labor dependency ratio averages, in table 2.1, reflect differences that are statistically significant among the three locales, demonstrating the greater mobilization of labor resources among the San Pedran households. The reason for this differentiation can be traced to the indigenous condition of the Guatemalan community, where socioethnic rationales of labor market insertion prevail. As has been shown in other studies of indigenous labor market insertion, these households tend to adopt strategies that maximize current income, incorporating most of the household members into the labor market (Pérez Sáinz, Bastos, and Camus 1992; Bastos and Camus 1998).[28] But labor insertion is different in each of the communities, since the various segments that have been identified have differing degrees of incidence in each locale. Thus, in La Fortuna, global employment significantly increases per capita income, but this does not happen in the case of modern employment. The opposite situation can be found in the Salvadoran case. And in San Pedro Sacatepéquez, global employment is significant, as is nonlocal. This diversity suggests various ideas. First, globalized employment does not always lead to an improvement in material welfare. Second, traditional occupations have little relevance for welfare, implying that these activities are marked by marginalization corresponding to an economy of poverty: the poor producing for the poor. Third, the relationship with modern employment is complex and refers to particularities in each universe. These observations imply that in each of the territories the three historical rationales that have been identified are in effect. Thus, traditional employment expresses the clearly subordinated situation of the rationale that sustains it. But in terms of the other two, the evidence on occupational structure does not show that globalization consistently plays a hegemonic role imposing itself on the corresponding national modernization.

Thus, we have a first general view of these three locales. Despite their insertion in globalized activities, poverty persists in all of them but to varying degrees, reflecting more the previous modernization processes and styles of each country. In other words, the nation still counts. However, integration has not been consolidated, since even in the communities with lower poverty levels, there are significant percentages of households at risk of falling into poverty. The factors associated with these (dis)integration dynamics are varied, and in differing ways. The sociodemographic dimensions appear to be universal even though they do not always produce the expected results. However, this universalization is nuanced, as is the case of education, which reflects the importance of the state in these locales and of the insertion of differing sociohistoric processes expressed in the current local dynamics. The specifics of each of the locales are reflected in the labor insertions of the households from a demand as well as supply point of view of the labor market. Regarding demand, differing sociocultural logics are at play in the universes that have to do with the degree of mobilization of labor resources in the households. In terms of supply, the interaction of differing socioproductive rationales leads to various configurations expressed in diverse occupational structures by locale. Explaining these distinctions leads us to the analysis of the respective labor markets in the next section.

LABOR MARKETS AND LABOR RATIONALES

As a first step in this direction, table 2.4 offers a profile of the supply side of the market with the main sociodemographic attributes of workers, as well as the demand side based on the analytical proposal of segmentation.

The upper part of this table refers to the respective supply of each labor market where two common traits can be seen among the three universes. These are labor markets that are not very masculine given the important presence of women. And, as expected, the average age reflects a mature labor force.[29] However, differences in terms of human capital reflect distinctions that have already been detected in the households, and these refer once again to national variations and the style of development followed in each country.

The lower part of the table refers to demand, of which different characteristics of the place of work have been combined with the occupational segmentation used in the previous section. Concretely, four occupational areas are considered. That called global refers to the selected activity in each locale: tourism in La Fortuna, apparel in San Pedro, and handicrafts in La Palma. The modern segment refers to all employment in establishments with more than five employees, in the public sector, or salaried workers who contribute to social security, regardless of the size of the business. The traditional segment includes the rest of the occupations. Each of these occupations refers only to positions located in the respective locale. Thus, we also take into account nonlocal employment, representing the fourth segment.[30]

Table 2.4. Labor Market Profiles by Locale

Dimensions	La Fortuna (n = 304)	La Palma (n = 416)	San Pedro Sacatepéquez (n = 616)	Total* (n = .336)	p <*
					.071
Sex (%)					
Male	63.8	55.3	58.9	58.9	
Female	36.2	44.7	41.1	41.1	
Age (average in years)	33.8	35.6	35.1	i34.9	.243
Educational level (average in years)	8.1	6.1	4.8	5.9	.000
Segments (%)					.000
Global	32.6	36.5	47.7	40.8	
Modern	33.6	14.8	2.3	13.3	
Traditional	29.2	40.2	30.8	33.4	
Nonlocal	4.6	8.5	19.2	12.5	

*Analysis of variance for metric variables and chi-squared for nonmetric variables.
Source: FLACSO survey.

Finished shirts at Villasa ready to be packaged and shipped to the maquila contractor. Villasa is one of the four largest factories in San Pedro Sacatepéquez, and as can be partially appreciated here, relatively large amounts of space are needed in order to obtain bigger direct contracts. This is a clear limitation for most of the smaller establishments that work out of their house.
Photo courtesy of Ricardo Ramírez Arriola.

Villasa workers, indigenous men and women, from San Pedro Sacatepéquez lining up on pay day.
Photo courtesy of Ricardo Ramírez Arriola.

Kaqchiquel women at the Villasa factory carrying out final quality control checks and sorting of finished shirts.
Photo courtesy of Ricardo Ramírez Arriola.

Kaqchiquel woman sewing shirt pieces at the Villasa factory in San Pedro Sacatepéquez. Both men and women, as can be seen in the background, participate in various phases of sewing.
Photo courtesy of Ricardo Ramírez Arriola.

La Fortuna shows a relatively even distribution of labor in the three local segments, while in La Palma traditional employment dominates. But
in San Pedro Sacatepéquez global employment has greater relevance.
Modern employment has little relevance, explained by two possible facts:
the proximity to the capital and the fact that modern employment refers
principally to that of apparel manufacturing through subcontracting that
has been redefined as global employment. In general terms, it could be
said that global employment absorbs a significant proportion of labor in
each of the locales. At the same time, nonlocal employment is significant
only in the Guatemalan case, which can be explained yet again by the
proximity of the community to the capital.

As we mentioned in the previous section, it is pertinent to justify our
proposed labor market segmentation. We start with the classic distinction between modern and traditional employment. In principle, this
refers to the segmentation between formal and informal that has dominated and continues to prevail in the literature in Latin America. However, a few observations are necessary. On the one hand, the terms
modern and *traditional* have a more pertinent historical connotation in
terms of our idea of the presence of different socioterritorial rationales.
On the contrary, *formal* and *informal* fundamentally refer to national
modernity. Obviously we are not proposing that traditional activities are
mere vestiges of the past. They have been redefined by the past modernity as they are in the current period of globalization. The same occurs
with modern employment, where this redefinition is much clearer in the
Guatemalan case. And on the other hand, our understanding of modern
employment combines the two interpretations present in the region concerning formal/informal. The extinct Program for Regional Employment
for Latin America and the Caribbean (PREALC) of the International Labor Organization (ILO) proposed that the segmentation came about in
terms of the market of goods. Thus, the distinction operated at the level
of the establishment based on the technological heterogeneity induced
by import substitution industrialization. In other words, this was a technological segmentation operationalized though the size of the establishment as a proxy variable of the relationship between capital and labor.[31]
On the other hand, there was the regulationist focus that emphasized
state action and its incidence in the labor market institutionalizing (or
not) employment relations. This focus presented the direct segmentation
of the labor market.[32] In another text, we have argued that both positions
have looked at different phenomena and thus are complementary rather
than competing analytical alternatives. The confusion has emerged due
to the use of the same term, *formal/informal*, in analyzing differing phenomena (Pérez Sáinz 1998). In this spirit, the focus adopted here combines operationally the basic ideas of both approaches: the size of the

establishment and labor regulation (operationalized as contributions to the national system of social security).

In addition, Latin American realities have suffered important changes in the last several years. The exhaustion of the previous model of development, expressed in the crisis of the 1980s and the application of structural adjustment programs, implies the formation of a new economic order. It appears that this tends to impose a model of accumulation based on export-oriented production, within the rationale of globalization dominating the world context. In this sense, it would be thought that the reflection concerning the issues related to informal/formal, and thus the segmentation of the labor market, should change. As has already been mentioned, the central criteria in the PREALC focus for differentiating the formal sector from the informal was the capital:labor ratio operationalized through the proxy variable of the size of the establishment according to the number of employees. However, given technological changes, an association of this sort between these two variables can no longer be made where it is assumed that larger establishments are more productive. This relationship corresponds to the Fordist productive world based on economies of scale and in-line production. The development of new technologies, especially microelectronic, means that these can be perfectly adapted to smaller firms; in other words, productivity is no longer a privilege of large businesses. But the regulationist focus also comes into question. It is incontestable that labor markets, the analytical reference point in this interpretation, are being subjected to a growing level of flexibility involving a generalized deregulation. From this perspective, this means that we face rampant informalization of employment in which the distinction between formal and informal progressively loses pertinence. The expression "informalization of formality" that tends to be used in this focus reflects this trend. However, this expression questions the heuristic capacity of this focus (Pérez Sáinz 1998).

In this sense, we find pertinent the consideration of a new and emerging segment that cannot be analyzed through the old categories and that we refer to as global employment. In other words, occupational heterogeneity in the current globalized modernization is more complex than in the past.

Finally, it is also important to separate out nonlocal employment. It is only in this way that we can talk about a local labor market. Historically, with national modernization, two types of dynamics were at work. The first had to do with the lack of employment in local economies bringing about migration in which the final destination point tended to be metropolitan areas. But there was also another dynamic that had to do with the integration of the local in the national space, bringing about the development of certain types of activities, especially in the area of services, and generating in this way new occupations and thus preventing some migration. Both dynamics were expressions of the configuration of a national labor market. Globalization questions this characterization. The emergence of global employment implies a revitalization of the local economy in which local occupational dynamics are guided more by global influences than the opportunities in the national labor market.

This phenomenon is linked to the de(re)territorialization that national labor markets suffer in globalization. This redefinition takes place on two levels: supra- and subnational. In terms of the first level, undoubtedly the main expression of this trend is transnational migration. In addition to its impacts in the household, this phenomenon presents two issues that deserve mention in terms of labor markets. The first has to do with the emigration of the labor force as a mechanism of adjustment in the labor market in some Latin American countries. The function of absorption of labor surplus, a role played in the past by the informal sector, is complemented now by emigration, given the increasing limitations for expansion of viable self-employment. In this way, migration acts as a true safety valve in labor markets with limited opportunities for employment. Additionally, the reception of remittances can impact the rates of labor participation, the levels of unemployment, levels of remuneration, and, consequently, the labor dynamics of sending countries (Funkhouser 1992a, 1992b). The second issue refers to the fact that this phenomenon transcends individuals and households, involving entire communities in the globalization process. This involves the transnationalization of communities, which implies three new trends with regard to previous migratory patterns.[33] First, it is a product of global capitalism since it responds to the demand for labor from the North. Second, it constitutes a distinctive social phenomenon from traditional migratory adaptation patterns. Third, it offers greater possibilities for popular initiatives (Portes et al. 1999). This affects not only those that transmigrate and their respective households but the entire community through participation in transmigratory dynamics, evolving into a different socioterritory in globalization.[34]

But transnationalization for the world of labor is not limited only to the transmigration of the labor force. There is another phenomenon that should also be equally considered: the transnationalization of collective labor action. In the previous model, trade union activities clearly reached only as far as the national borders given the spatial relationship with the state, making it a sociopolitical actor (Touraine 1988). The development of new global activities has brought about not only the transnationalization of economic activities but also sociopolitical ones. In certain global chains, especially those that are buyer driven,[35] a new collective action is emerging with certain new traits. In the first place, this action does not circumscribe itself to national spaces due to the transnational nature of the chain itself, involving local (national) as well as nonlocal actors. Second, non-labor actors such as NGOs, women's organizations (in some of these industries, the labor force is predominantly feminine, and thus gender is an unavoidable dimension), or consumer organizations are present. This last group is important, since given the type of chain, the consumer market in the North is fundamentally an area of action of symbolic nature (specifically, the image of the trademark), which takes on great importance. Additionally, globalization tends to depict consumers, along with firms, as the main actors. In this way, labor contradictions in the lower ends of the chain, where capital dominates labor, can manifest themselves in the final market with asymmetries that are not so favorable for the businesses. And thus new instruments for action emerge such as monitoring and codes of conduct (Koepke, Molina, and Quinteros 2000; Quinteros 2000). This is a first attempt at moralizing global economic life.

The subnational reterritorialization has brought about a redefinition in the classic spatial dimensions of the previous modernity in the opposition between urban (modern) and rural (traditional). Since the crisis decade of the 1980s, territorial redistribution of activities and employment can be detected, and this spatial dimension is less clear (Tardanico and Menjívar Larín 1997). New points of view on rural development consider that the local economy has emerged as the crucial analytical unit where the relationships between urban centers and rural markets are critical (Shejtman 1999). This redefines the horizon of the rural labor markets in a much more complex manner than in the past. In this same vein, it can be said that rural employment can no longer be reduced to agrarian employment. Rather, as has been documented in Central America, a growing part of rural household income comes from nonagrarian activities (Weller 1997). This questions the historical continuity of the peasantry as a relevant actor in globalized modernity (Martínez 1999). But there is also a subnational reterritorialization taking place due to the fragmentation of the national labor market with the budding of local markets, the fruit of this revitalization which is paradoxically induced by globalization, as mentioned in the previous chapter. For this reason, it is important to separate nonlocal employment to compare it with the local labor dynamics.

With these analytical precisions and returning to our empirical evidence, we try to link the supply (sociodemographic attributes of the labor force) with the demand (labor segmentation) of these labor markets in terms of the price of this type of market (and the main reason people participate in them): income. This is done through another multivariable[36] analysis comparing the three universes under consideration (see table 2.5).

Before beginning an interpretation of the results, we need to review, if even briefly, the first variable: number of hours worked per week. This

Table 2.5. Multiple Linear Regression Models of the Decimal Logarithm of Income Based on Selected Variables by Locale

Variable	La Fortuna	La Palma	San Pedro Sacatepéquez
Number of hours worked per week	.003*	.004**	.004**
	(.001)	(.001)	(.001)
Women	−.138**	−.179**	−.068
	(.045)	(.045)	(.037)
Age	.004	.003	−.004*
	(.002)	(.002)	(.002)
Educational level	.023**	.024**	.026**
	(.005)	(.005)	(.004)
Years of seniority	.019*	.021**	.008
	(.008)	(.005)	(.005)
(Years of seniority)^2	−.0006*	−.0006**	−.002
	(.000)	(.000)	(.000)
Household head	.039	.064	.159**
	(.044)	(.048)	(.039)
Global employment	.196**	−.010	.233**
	(.051)	(.052)	(.042)
Modern employment	.038	.245**	.224*
	(.051)	(.069)	(.112)
Nonlocal employment	.212*	.168*	.225**
	(.051)	(.078)	(.051)
Constant	4.438**	2.507**	2.405**
	(.102)	(.095)	(.099)
Adjusted R^2	.226	.334	.261
F	.000	.000	.000
N	270	319	484

*$p < .05$.
**$p < .01$.
Source: FLACSO survey.

variable could have been incorporated into the dependent variable by using income per hour. This approach would have involved an interpretation of this dimension on the demand side of the labor market in terms of how the establishments manage the remuneration of their labor. By keeping this variable as an independent factor, hours worked is considered as a function of the availability of time by the workers. In other words, supply is privileged, which is what interests us since with this analytical approach to the labor market we are trying to develop a better understanding of the rationale of household labor insertion. Thus, a high hourly wage does not necessarily imply a large monthly income since this could correspond to a reduced workday. What is of interest, for the material reproduction of the domestic unit, is the total amount obtained by each of the employed members. The results show that, as was expected, this variable is significant in each of the universes, but what is interesting to highlight is the lower incidence in La Fortuna. Our hypothesis concerning this point reflects again the incidence of the national in the local in terms of the existence of an active policy of minimum wages present in Costa Rica, even during the crisis period of the 1980s (Pérez Sáinz 1999b). In this same regard, it can be considered that the use of the labor force in the Costa Rican universe is more productive and less intensive than in the other two locales.

Continuing with the supply side, in two of the universes women are more poorly remunerated than men: 14 percent less in La Fortuna and 18 percent less in La Palma. Only in the Guatemalan locale do we have a labor market where gender inequalities have been overcome in terms of remuneration.

Age is only significant in the case of San Pedro Sacatepéquez, but this observation implies the recognition of younger workers, probably for their higher energy levels. In other words, it is a labor market that privileges an intense use of the labor force.

Concerning human capital, there are two points to make. First, in terms of the formal component, educational attainment, this is a very robust factor as well as a universal one, reaffirming what has already been stated in terms of education. Second, the other nonformal component, experience, refers to only the length of time in the current position. Thus, as an indicator of labor experience, it is limited but also shows occupational stability. The aspect we wish to emphasize is the first. Since the majority of establishments in the three universes cannot formally be considered businesses, we posit that this experience does not reflect labor mobility within the labor market but rather craft trajectories. In this regard, there are differing results. Labor experience is recognized in La Fortuna and even more so in La Palma, while the contrary is found in San Pedro Sacatepéquez. This last result is a bit perplexing, taking into account two factors: (1) this is an indigenous community where it would be thought that labor experience, accumulated over time, would be recognized; (2) of the three cases considered, this community is the one where the respective globalized activity has a longer history, and thus one would hope to find more defined and sustained labor trajectories over time. Thus, in this locale, we suggest that certain dynamics erode the impact of labor experience (discussed in the next chapter).

The dimension of head of household is only significant in San Pedro Sacatepéquez. This suggests that family hierarchies are reflected and reaffirmed in the labor market but only in this universe, and that in the other two, intrafamily dynamics are less cohesive due to this disassociation. This phenomenon is related to the fact that this is an indigenous community. In other words, it appears that the more cohesive dynamics of the family group in this culture means that the principal source of income is generated by the person identified as the head of the household, thus reinforcing his authority (this is not a gender lapse but rather a specific reinforcement of the authority of male-headed households).

In terms of factors associated with demand, we have to compare the three segments[37] among themselves since they present mutually exclusive opportunities of employment. This means that the interpretation of the results must be done by locale.

La Fortuna shows that the most attractive option for employment, from the point of view of remuneration, is employment in the tourism sector, reaffirming that this is a globalized community. The second option is to work outside the district, but the number of people who do so is minimal, and thus this is not a relevant issue. But analytically the most interesting question is related to why modern employment is not attractive. It is important to remember that we are talking about Costa Rica, where the modernization of the labor market took place earlier and is the most generalized in Central America (Pérez Sáinz 1999b). In this regard, the paradigmatic occupation of national modernization has been public employment, the weight of which is very limited. Because there are few public jobs, along with the dynamism of tourism, this segment is not an attractive option. This phenomenon implies that this locale cannot be characterized as having a high level of institutional development—something that is not strange given the centralism of the Costa Rican state, accentuated in the case of La Fortuna since it is only a district and not a cantón.

The opposite situation is found in La Palma. Modern employment is the most attractive option, while handicrafts are not. This last finding makes relative the condition of globalization in this community and presents a series of questions concerning the handicraft activity, which will be addressed in the next chapter. Nonlocal employment is the second option, but only 10 percent of the labor force is employed in this segment: in other words, this situation is not of importance. In terms of modern employment, contrary to the Costa Rican case, a third of those occupied in this segment correspond to the public sector. This is a reflection of the increased presence of the national state on a local level in El Salvador and a more developed institutionality.

As in La Fortuna, global employment appears to be the most attractive option in San Pedro Sacatepéquez. Thus, this is also a globalized locale. But nonlocal employment is of equal importance. We have already mentioned the proximity to the metropolitan area of Guatemala City as an explanation of the trend (and the nonsignificant result of modern employment, with very little incidence, is also related to the proximity of the capital). But what is interesting is that half of the nonlocal employment corresponds to small merchants, who are mostly self-employed. This is a prolonging of the apparel activity through which modernization of the locale started and implies that despite globalized subcontracting, the previous socioproductive rationale continues. The corollary to this is that we will probably find a heterogeneous socioproductive fabric in the productive agglomeration of this locale.[38]

To deepen our understanding of the labor market dynamics, it is important to analyze the sociolabor differences within each locale to see how these are expressed within the respective globalized activity. The results of this exercise can be found in table 2.6, which reflects the levels of employment access and income gaps between traditionally vulnerable sociolabor groups, contrasting the globalized segment with the rest of the local activities in order to establish which generates more labor inequities.

In terms of access, the results show a common pattern among the three universes: young people have greater levels of access in the respective globalized activity. The same cannot be said of women, where the results are mixed: an important level of access in tourism, no significant differences in the Salvadoran community, and less access in apparel manufacturing when compared with other activities in the Guatemalan case. Nicaraguan labor has a similar weight in occupational areas in the Costa Rican locale, while in San Pedro Sacatepéquez, there is a greater proportion of indigenous labor in apparel manufacturing than in other sectors.

In terms of income gaps,[39] the first thing to point out is that we have also included a comparison between workers and owners of production; in other words, we want to look at class inequalities. This is the only phenomenon that is common among all three of the locales and activities, highlighting particularly the case of tourism in La Fortuna and non-handicraft activities in La Palma as those areas where this inequality is the greatest. The other category subjected to income inequalities, although not in all cases, is female labor: activities other than tourism in the Costa Rican locale, both occupational options in the Salvadoran universe, and nonapparel manufacturing in San Pedro Sacatepéquez. Young people also face this sort of inequality but only in non-tourist-related activities in La Fortuna. And the two specific groups (Nicaraguans in Costa Rica and indigenous in the Guatemalan case) do not appear to be paid lower wages.

Thus, in terms of access, it appears that the globalized occupations contribute to reducing historic inequalities. However, in terms of income gaps and with the exception of class, the evidence is mixed, and thus nonconclusive.

With this deeper understanding of the labor markets and the labor rationales that these express, we can revisit the broader view of the local dynamics from the household.

Table 2.6. Access to Employment and Income Gaps by Sociolabor Category, Segments, and Locale

Sociolabor Dimensions	La Fortuna		La Palma		San Pedro Sacatepéquez	
	Tourism	Nontourism	Handicrafts	Nonhandicrafts	Apparel	Nonapparel
Access						
Women (%)	45.5*	33.0*	51.7	45.5	33.1**	58.6**
Young people (%)[a]	38.4*	25.7*	34.1**	21.1**	38.6**	18.7**
Nicaraguan (%)	18.2	13.6				
Indigenous (%)					90.8**	79.3**
Gaps						
Women	−2.8	−15.6*	21.7**	−11.4*	−5.3	−21.76**
Young people[a]	−15.6*	−3.1	−5.3	−1.4	2.3	15.3
Nicaraguan	−8.5	−4.9				
Indigenous					−5.8	−11.6
Workers	−50.4**	−36.0**	−31.5	−64.0**	−32.6**	−48.5**

[a]Less than twenty-four years of age.
*p < .05.
**p < .01.
Source: FLACSO survey.

LOCAL DYNAMICS: A VIEW FROM THE SOCIAL

This overview must be approached separately by community, but within each interpretation, various analytically relevant problems will stand out and transcend the particularities of each universe.

In the case of La Fortuna, social integration clearly prevails, but a third of the households that are not poor are at risk of falling into poverty. The predominance of social integration does not establish differences between the local population and Nicaraguan immigrants, and it rests solidly on the factor of education. These two phenomena are reproduced in the labor market in addition to clearly demonstrating that women face wage discrimination. Global employment emerges as the most attractive occupational option and the most solid for guaranteeing the material welfare in the households in La Fortuna, while traditional occupations have a greatly reduced impact. In other words, investment in education and maximizing the number of household members, preferably men, who work in tourism appear to be key elements in obtaining social integration in this case.

In La Palma, the majority of households are integrated, but this is not as universalized as in the Costa Rican case; however, the risk of impoverishment, while not unimportant, is not as significant. The dynamics of social integration are also clearly linked to education but complemented by migration through the reception of remittances. The impact of education lessens where work experience is also of equal importance in the labor market. In other words, this is an environment where human capital is recognized in different facets, but this is not the case in terms of gender, where women are discriminated against. Modern employment, with an important proportion of public employment, is the most attractive option. Thus, the material welfare of the households depends on investment in education, as in the Costa Rican case, but the labor insertion strategy, also favoring men, is oriented toward modern employment; additionally, if remittances are sent, transnational migration becomes a key factor in overcoming poverty.

In the case of San Pedro Sacatepéquez, poverty continues to be generalized but without ethnic differentiation. However, this discrimination still exists in the labor market but is not transferred into the domestic units since the majority of indigenous households opt for a strategy of maximizing the labor resources through their insertion. Women are not discriminated against in terms of remuneration, and heads of household and younger workers are favored. As in the Costa Rican case, global employment is the most attractive option, along with nonlocal employment made possible by the proximity to the capital. Thus, to overcome poverty, the San Pedran households invest in education (although its importance is not nearly as significant as in the other two cases); labor strategies, privileging heads of household and young people, are more diversified, incorporating employment in apparel manufacturing as well as work outside the community.

This set of social practices used by households in each of the three locales considered to obtain social integration can be reinterpreted in terms of three basic rationales, mentioned in the previous chapter, configuring the communities. This reinterpretation will assist in identifying key analytical issues that will be taken up in the next chapter.

In the first place, in terms of traditional rationales, there are several interpretations. First, evidently employment that has been termed traditional is only relevant in La Fortuna, and even at that, is limited. Second, there is a massive incorporation of household members into the labor market in San Pedro Sacatepéquez that tends to neutralize the effects of demographic dependency. It can be considered that the traditional peasant behavior of mobilization of labor as a family resource, rather than an individual one, is still present in this community. This is accentuated among indigenous households. Thus, traditional employment has a limited impact and probably plays a secondary role in the local dynamics. However, it is important to remember that national as well as globalized modernizations have come to rest on the primary socioterritoriality of the neighborhood community based on a traditional historic period. In other words, tradition is prolonged but redefined in later historic periods.

The impact of national modernization is mainly expressed through the dimension of education, which, as has been seen, is one of the most solid foundations for social integration in the three universes. These educational advances are mainly a result of national public policies. In other words, despite the structural adjustment programs and their objective of state reduction, the state continues to be present. Obviously, its activities are linked to the type of national modernization adopted in each of the three countries, and this leads to a reflection, although brief, about the modes of national modernization.

It is well known that marked differences are evident in terms of the modernization options implemented as a result of the oligarchic crisis affecting Central America during the 1930s (Torres Rivas 1984, 1987; Bulmer-Thomas 1989). The dominant sectors in Guatemala and El Salvador embarked on an exclusionary modernization through the installation of authoritarian regimes. Generalized impoverishment, especially in rural areas, together with state terrorism brought about civil wars. However, in Costa Rica the road taken was democratic, and, since the end of the 1940s, the mode of modernization was inclusive, leading to the universalization of social citizenship. In other words, the historical logic of each society is also reflected in each of these communities. Thus, globalization does not lead to a drastic rupture with the previous modernization; rather, their effects continue to fundamentally determine the social dynamics of the locales. In other words, the past, through the state and the nation, continues to count and should not be forgotten.

But the modernizing rationales present two other issues. On the one hand, there is the importance of public employment in La Palma, becoming one of the main pillars for social integration and, on the other hand, the occupation of choice. The relative weight of public activities within the sector introduces the issue of institutionality. It is in this sense that La Palma presents itself as being perhaps the universe where more development has taken place in this direction, something that would be much more limited in the Costa Rican case. This contrast can also be noted in the differing processes of decentralization in these two countries. For its part, in San Pedro Sacatepéquez, the proximity of the capital would imply that institutionality is subsumed through the capital due to this peculiar socioterritory. In other words, there are differing types of institutional development, whose causes will need to be explored.

Moreover, in San Pedro Sacatepéquez national modernization is also expressed through nonlocal employment. As was shown previously, the important issue here relates to the persistence of the self-employed commercial sellers. This was precisely the activity that inaugurated the modernization of the community. In other words, this tradition, generated through the national modernization, continues. This leads to a juxtaposition within the activities of apparel manufacturing of modern rationales with those that are global; in this regard, within this cluster a heterogeneous socioproductive fabric is implied. But at that same time, this persistence can face a counterargument, from the preceding section, relating to the nonrecognition of labor experience and age in the labor market in this locale. In other words, tradition is not recognized, and this implies that in this locale community capital, understood as the effects of sociocultural resources in the economic behavior of individuals, is questioned. Thus, this central analytical issue must be analyzed not only in the Guatemalan case but in the other two as well.

Finally, the globalizing logics show their strength through employment in the cases of La Fortuna and San Pedro Sacatepéquez, where they are determining factors in the dynamics of household social integration. In fact, we may say that the respective globalized activities have emerged as the main foundation in the local economy. This phenomenon, however, does not take place in the Salvadoran case, where globalization expresses itself through migration, which is without a doubt the main means of global insertion in this country. Thus, it must be asked why tourism and manufacturing subcontracting are globalized activities with positive impacts while handicrafts is not. In other words, there can be multiple effects of globalization, and the type of activity and the means of insertion into the global market count.

Thus, the view from the social perspective shows us that the interaction between the distinct rationales (traditional, modern, and global) as they are made up in each community express themselves in differing outcomes. This reinterpretation reveals a series of important issues: the persistence of the past expressed through the presence of the national and the state in the current local dynamics; the differing institutional configurations and the processes that generate them; the heterogeneity of the socioproductive fabric of the clusters that place the locales in the global market; the tendencies that cross community capital and their consequences in the economic behaviors in the face of globalization; the diversity of insertions in this process and their consequences in term of community cohesion. All of these issues that have emerged from this discussion of the social view establish the framework for the analytical approach in the next chapter.

NOTES

1. In the political-administrative configuration of Costa Rica, the cantón is synonymous with the municipal district of El Salvador and Guatemala. A cantón is composed of various districts that are the primary political-administrative unit.

2. We use the term *establishment* rather than *firm* when referring to the diverse economic units in the communities since this is a more generic term and includes economic units with a subsistence orientation as well as those with an entrepreneurial rationale.

3. The business owners of La Fortuna consider that tourists need to stay for at least three nights to enjoy all the attractions of the area.

4. In and around the community are various establishments for lodging, ranging in quality.

5. This seed is about the size of a large grape. The exterior part is dark brown, but the interior is white, and it is upon this that the artists paint or sculpt. It is said that the discovery of this seed for artistic purposes was made when Fernando Llort and a group of friends were conversing and observed a boy scraping the seed on the cement. When the interior was revealed, the strength of its whiteness impressed the artists, who immediately began to imagine the seed's aesthetic possibilities.

6. This is the Mayan group that has historically occupied the territory where this community is located.

7. According to the Spanish language dictionary of the *Real Academia Español* (21st ed.), a *caballería* is an agrarian measurement equaling approximately 3,863 areas, the equivalent of 3.863 hectares. A *legua* is 3,105.5 hectares.

8. As Falla (1978) showed in his classic study of San Antonio de Ilotenango in El Quiché, it was the community sectors linked to commerce and transportation

that, together with the support of Catholic Action, led to the modernizing changes in the communities.

9. This man also served as a Mayan priest, demonstrating his identification with the indigenous world, as well as having directed a social development program linked to the peace accords and having been a presidential candidate for a leftist coalition in the 1999 elections.

10. The data are the product of household surveys carried out in each of the locales. The characteristics of the surveys can be consulted in the methodological appendix.

11. This method of measuring the poverty line (a static measurement of the situation of households limited to wage and nonwage income) has well-known limits, but for our purposes, using the poverty line is the most appropriate methodology since it relates material welfare in the household with the labor market, introducing the issues related to the clusters, given that the majority of income in the domestic unit comes from employment.

12. Another author who has insisted on this direction is Roberts (1996, 1998).

13. This virtue has also been pointed out by Faría (1995).

14. This author also proposes using the combined method of measuring poverty (the poverty line as well as unsatisfied basic needs) to identify this group.

15. The idea of reflexive modernity is also shared by Giddens and Lash, although with conceptions that do not always converge (Beck, et al. 1997).

16. Obviously the results in each country have been very different. National differences can be explained by the moment initiated, the rhythm of modernization, and the coalitions formed around this project.

17. One can think of El Salvador and the incredible improvement in indicators related to impoverishment and the distribution of income during the 1990s. These are surprising changes, leading to the hypothesis that they are the result of migrant remittances. The opposite has taken place in countries like Ecuador and Argentina where accounts, including dollar accounts, have been frozen, leading to the impoverishment of sectors of the middle class.

18. This is the case of Costa Rica, where a real increase in wages occurred in the labor market during the 1990s.

19. The details of the estimation of the risk of poverty line can be consulted in the appendix.

20. Concretely, these are linear multiple regression models whose specifications can be found in the appendix.

21. For an initial approximation concerning the new family arrangements in Central America, see Cordero (1998).

22. We will mention here that *modern* employment refers to nonglobalized local employment in establishments that are not small and have regulated labor relations. *Traditional* employment is also nonglobalized local employment but in small establishments without regulation.

23. The adjective *modern* refers to the national modernization period.

24. In fact, in the San Pedro Sacatepéquez model, if we substitute the demographic dependency ratio for that of labor, the coefficient is just as significant as in the Costa Rican case.

25. The cross-tabulation between this variable and poverty does not produce statistically significant results in any of the three universes, either.

26. In terms of the general population, the distances are reduced since the average in the Costa Rica case is lower (6.4), while it is higher in the Guatemalan (4.5) and Salvadoran (5.1) cases. It is interesting to highlight the advances made in this last country since primary educational results are overtaking those of Costa Rica, reflecting the deterioration of education in this country that has historically been characterized by its relatively high level of social development (Programa de las Naciones Unidas para el Desarrollo 1999, table 6.6).

27. Models using the specific variables were also processed: households headed by Nicaraguans in La Fortuna to capture the presence of this population; remittances in La Palma to reflect transnational migration, a generalized phenomenon in El Salvador; and households headed by the indigenous in San Pedro Sacatepéquez to show the ethnic composition of this community. Of these variables, only that related to remittances in the case of La Palma showed a level of incidence, marking this as one of the main modes of insertion of El Salvador in globalization, can be found in the universe under consideration. In the other cases, however (the presence of Nicaraguans in La Fortuna and ethnicity in San Pedro Sacatepéquez), statistical significance was not found. In other words, these specific factors are relativized in these two cases. But in bivariate cross-tabulations of these variables with poverty, Nicaraguan households in La Fortuna have twice the level of poverty as compared with Costa Rican. But where the association is much clearer is in terms of ethnicity in the Guatemalan locale, showing the higher levels of poverty among indigenous households. However, these two associations are no longer significant when controlled by other variables.

28. These studies refer to the metropolitan area of Guatemala City and are pertinent for the current analysis for two reasons: San Pedro Sacatepéquez stopped being an agricultural community several decades ago, and it is close to the capital.

29. The medians in the three universes coincide: thirty-three years old.

30. See the appendix for an explanation of the operationalization of these variables.

31. Mezzera (1987) offers an elegant explanation of this segmentation in terms of the oligopolistic behavior of large firms in Latin America from the previous modernization.

32. Portes is the figure that stands out here and whose main works on the topic have been compiled in Portes (1995). It is also important to mention the innovative application of this analytical framework by Itzigsohn (2000) in his comparison between Costa Rica and the Dominican Republic.

33. In this regard, it is important to refer to the pertinent distinction of Pries (2000) among immigration (integration into the receiving society), remigration (return to the place of origin), and transmigration. This last situation refers to family networks with a plurilocal transnational social space.

34. See the reflections that we have developed in the second part of chapter 1 on transnational migration as a scenario for interaction between the global and the local.

35. The chains can be producer or buyer driven. The buyer-driven ones that involve nondurable consumer goods (clothing, shoes, toys, etc.) define power relations that make up the chain in relation to the market. In chapter 4, we will consider the issue of global chains.

36. We use three multiple linear regression models detailed in the appendix.

37. The excluded segment and the one included in the constant is traditional employment. This decision corresponds to the relatively low incidence of this type of employment in the material welfare of the household, as was observed in the previous sections.

38. As in the case of the households, specific variables were processed in each of the universes. The consideration related to Nicaraguan nationality in La Fortuna did not produce differences in remuneration. However, this was not the case in terms of ethnicity in the Guatemalan case, where historic patterns of socio-ethnic discrimination continue to be present, and the indigenous receive 10 percent less than nonindigenous workers.

39. The values are the coefficients from regressions that are specified in the appendix.

40. Within this category are all the occupational categories except owners and self-employed laborers whose income is equal to or greater than that of the median of the owners.

3

Clusters, Community Capital, and Institutionality

The analysis carried out in the previous chapter has brought up a series of issues that will be addressed in this one. Three broad topics incorporate these various issues. The first refers to the clusters where the socioproductive fabric will be examined through a double optic: in terms of heterogeneity, and based on its cohesion through the existence of external economies that permits us to be able to discuss the clusters. The second section refers to the topic of community capital. We broach this topic separately for two reasons. First, because while this concept deals with economic behavior, and therefore could be included in the discussion on clusters, its origins are sociocultural in nature. In fact, it is this topic that makes the community context visible and is a fundamental part of our methodological interest. Second, it is a topic that serves as a bridge between clusters and institutions. Finally, the third section deals with the manifestations of collective action as related to the globalized activity detected in each locale and the institutional configurations that exist, interpreting them in terms of whether they function with regard to the clusters.

CLUSTERS, SOCIOPRODUCTIVE HETEROGENEITY, AND EXTERNAL ECONOMIES

The descriptions of the genesis of each of the universes, at the beginning of the second chapter, permit us to speak of the existence of clusters in the sense that there is a territorial concentration of establishments belonging to the same type of activity. But we need to inquire about the nature of these clusters. Based on the evidence thus far, we may make a few general points.

The first has to do with the case of tourism as a cluster of services and thus not based on the production of goods. It should be remembered that the discussion on clusters is, in a certain way and for our type of realities, a representation of the old discussion on the development potential of small industry (Schmitz 1995). Thus, it is necessary to broaden the notion to all types of activities, especially tourism, which in many countries of the South plays a growing role given the sustained growth of this activity as one of the most dynamic within the new global order.

The second issue emerges from the contrast between the Guatemalan and Salvadoran cases, which are universes of industrial production. In the first case, it obviously implies the existence of manufacturing production, while in the second, it is more artisan in nature. In this sense, it is pertinent to refer to attempts to create typologies of clusters. From the prolific bibliography on industrial districts appearing between the end of the 1980s to the beginning of the 1990s, Markusen (1994) proposed the existence of four types of industrial districts:

- the *Italian* or *Marshallian* type, made up of small businesses with cooperative linkages;
- *central-radius*, organized in terms of large businesses that bring with them their suppliers;
- *platform-satellite*, structured on a base of related multinational firms that function as an enclave with respect to the local medium;
- and the districts that emerge from activities cultivated by *governmental* or *private institutions*.

Our cases unequivocally belong to the first type. For Latin America, Altenburg and Meyer-Stamer (1999) have proposed three types of clusters. The first is called survival clusters of micro- and small-scale enterprises with little interbusiness cooperation or specialization and oriented toward the national market. The second refers to clusters that grew out of the industrial import substitution period, of businesses with mass and differentiated production. The third refers to more recent dynamics generated by multinational firms that attract suppliers that locate nearby. It is also worthwhile to review McCormick's (1999) proposal based on African experiences, suggesting three types of clusters: groundwork clusters with micro- and small enterprises that compete among themselves without cooperative relationships (similar to the first type of the German authors); industrializing clusters with more advanced units also oriented to the national market; and complex industrial clusters where the market diversifies toward exports. Ironically, this latter typology, despite a more distant point of reference, turns out to be more pertinent for classification of the realities of San Pedro Sacatepéquez and La Palma. The Guatemalan case corresponds to the industrializing and the Salvadoran to the groundwork type. However, both orient most of their production toward exports. Thus, it would appear that the generalization of typologies with respect to clusters is limited by the pluridimensional nature, implying multiple combinations. In this sense, it is of more heuristic use to identify a series of key dimensions to characterize clusters ad hoc without placing them in a limited typological box.

In this sense, table 3.1 shows the profiles of the establishments,[1] where the sociodemographic characteristics of the proprietor are also taken into consideration. This consideration is justified for two reasons. First, the economic units, due to the fact that most are a result of self-employment, carry the stamp of the person who took the initiative in its formation. Second, the vast majority of the owners directly participate in the labor process.

With the exception of age, which shows that the owners, as expected, are mature, the rest of the dimensions appear to reflect differences that allow for a discussion on the various profiles.

La Fortuna is the universe in which women have greater access to ownership of the establishments. Educational levels are also higher, a fact linked to the national educational levels and a phenomenon that has

Table 3.1. Establishment Profiles by Locale

Dimensions	La Fortuna (n = 49)	La Palma (n = 48)	San Pedro Sacatepéquez (n = 50)
Women (%)	44.9	31.3	0.0
Age (average in years)	37.1	38.0	38.8
Educational level (average in years)	9.9	7.3	7.8
Experience (average in years)	7.6	14.6	17.3
Number of employees (average)	4.3	11.1	15.1
Location (%)			
In house	14.4	81.3	74.0
Separate locale	83.6	18.7	26.0
Other	2.0	0.0	0.0
Accounting (%)			
Formal	14.3	83.4	46.0
Informal	85.7	16.6	54.0

Source: Case studies of FLACSO.

already been emphasized in the previous chapter. The level of experience in the trade is lower than in the other two cases. The starting point of this activity does not seem to be the possible cause, since this occurred at about the same time as the handicraft activities in La Palma, which has an average number of years of experience in the workshop that is practically double. The lower number of employees also stands out and is probably due to the fact that this activity is not manufacturing but rather services. It must also be highlighted that the majority of cases entail a separation between the establishment and the house, leading to the conclusion that in these types of establishments they have overcome one of the principal manifestations of subsistence-oriented activities. It is also the universe where there are clearer indicators of entrepreneurial rationales, evidenced by the generalized use of formal accounting.[2]

In the case of La Palma, the most notorious characteristics concern two dimensions. First, it is the universe where most of the establishments are located within the house, and thus the handicraft activities appear to be subordinated as to the subsistence rationales of the household. Second, it is the case where we have found fewer entrepreneurial rationales. In other words, it appears to be the cluster where there is less economic modernization.

The traits that are detected in San Pedro Sacatepéquez are several. The most important is that women are not proprietors. We attribute this phenomenon to the fact that this is an indigenous community where public space is fundamentally occupied by men and, given that many of the establishments are familiar, it is the man as the head of household who appears as the owner. In this regard, it is important to point out that this gendered division has its origins at the beginning of the modernization in this community, when San Pedran men sold clothing from the capital throughout the country while the women stayed in the community space, secluded in the home. Two other traits to highlight are the higher levels of experience in the trade, which has to do with the fact that the activity in this universe dates back further, and the higher average in the number of employees. Actually, we are talking about four establishments that have more than fifty workers. In other words, in this cluster medium and large businesses have formed, depending on the criteria used, and thus this is a socioproductive fabric with greater levels of heterogeneity as compared to the other two, an issue mentioned in the previous chapter.

In this Guatemalan universe, the productive heterogeneity is also expressed in the manner in which work is organized and the technology used among the establishments.

In terms of the division of labor, prior to subcontracting through maquilas, the workshops were organized in a way in which each worker made a complete product. In other words, the division of labor was pre-

Taylorist. With the system of subcontracting, since the end of the 1980s, the workshops began to organize under the in-line work system, or Taylorist-type operations. But today there are workshops that have introduced the post-Taylorist-inspired modular system. However, the majority of establishments use in-line production where each person is dedicated to a single activity. One of the leading producers learned the advantages of the new system in a course through the Exporters Association[3] and pointed out that "currently a lot of plants use only the modular system, eliminating free time, but the workers must have incentives. There is a different treatment, consciousness raising of the people, to take better advantage of it. This requires a total restructuring of the workshop, more machines, so that time is not wasted; more space is needed and more training."

The difference between the modular system and the in-line one is that the operations begin and end in the same circle. People are not placed in a row, moving pile to pile until the task is finished. The machines must move, and the module is organized according to the clothing to be made. The number of people involved in the module depends on the number of operations used in making the piece of clothing. For example, another one of the leading producers points out that for making the pieces of clothing he manufactures, there are twenty-three operations in addition to packing. In the modular system, the same person can do two operations, and in this way packaging is not saturated and can begin earlier, while production continues. This person mentioned that "the problem with the in-line system is inventories, lost time in moving piles, you can't see if people are wasting time. . . . The advantage [with the modular system] is that the product is finished each day; inventory is not left over or money [is not] circulating in the shop."

The difficulty that these manufacturers confront is the adaptation of workers to this system since it requires a different outlook as well as maintaining or improving wages. In other words, the relationship with workers must change. This implies new entrepreneurial mentalities as tried by the board of one of the four existing factories in the community. One of the managers mentioned, "There we learned how competition is on an international level, especially for managers, generating changes in the business in order to be competitive in the year 2000. I went to a seminar on small and medium businesses, and there we connected up with other courses—changing the productive process, the way we treat people, being ready for the new millennium, being on top of things."

The reference to the division of labor refers to the type of technology used. In this respect, to make a shirt, for example, requires five different machines: an industrial sewing machine, a buttonhole maker, a buttoner, an overlock, and an arm closer. These are Japanese machines usually sold by Koreans in the capital. "The more diverse the machines one has, the more possibilities there are for getting different clients," says one of the producers. The technology has changed rapidly in the last seven or eight years. New technology is incorporated through market pressure via the contracting businesses, some of which provide access to machinery and its use, the value of which is deducted from the contract. This support is limited to producers with a direct contract and some of the larger subcontracting workshops. In other words, it appears that there are subcontracting cases whose linkages are less vertical and more cooperative. Learning how to use the machines is done in the workshop, but the workers have to know how to use at least the industrial sewing machine or overlocks. Among the different producers, they learn how to make different styles. It is also possible to visit different machine distributors and see their functions. The San Pedrans see no difficulty in incorporating tools or machinery, but this process is slightly behind the most advanced technology that the large factories use (especially in the capital), since their ability to renovate, due to the expense, is not the same. The leading producers interviewed coincide in pointing out that they have a greater capacity for production than what they currently are doing. In other words, they are experiencing underused capacity.

One of these people related:

> when we began we had old machines, ones that were fixed up or reconstructed even though they were industrial. Over time, all of these machines where changed, and we bought new ones. But even with this, this machinery is out-of-date. The cutting-edge technology, the most advanced that there is now, is not what we have, the computerized ones. We can make the same shirts, but we can't compete with the new technology that is computerized and programmed. Our technology is only halfway. We should also be training but once we get the machinery. What we have now is Japanese technology—there is a distributor in Guatemala. The machines we have were sent to us from the United States without paying taxes. . . . We learned watching; they taught us in the Van Heusen factory here in Guatemala—how to cut, how to make, how to pack, how to export. They have also given us loans for machinery.

Summarizing the table in question, in terms of economic modernization it would appear that La Palma is the universe with the least development contrasted with the case of La Fortuna, while San Pedro Sacatepéquez would be situated in between. This brings to us to the question of the heterogeneity of these clusters.

While these clusters are made up of small establishments, the fruit of self-employment rationales, there may be processes of differentiation with the development of medium and larger businesses. But at the same time we cannot assume that all small businesses are the same. In regard to this point, it is pertinent to review the old discussion on the heterogeneity of what used to constitute the informal phenomenon. This type of cluster represents one of the main manifestations of self-employment in globalization. The phenomenon, as we have argued in other texts (Pérez Sáinz 1998) should not be understood through the concept of informality, whose analytical pertinence should be limited to the previous modernizing period. But, since both phenomena are expressions, in different historic moments, of the logic of self-employment, certain reflections on informality continue to be valid for clusters of small businesses. So, contrary to homogenizing viewpoints that understood informality as synonymous with microenterprise, characterized by its accumulative potential repressed by legal obstacles by the state,[4] the need to identify distinct rationales that crossed informality was postulated: the accumulative as well as those oriented toward subsistence and, therefore, expressing only simple reproduction of the establishments (Pérez Sáinz 1991). This distinction seems to be relevant for the clusters since it will help profile the heterogeneity of the socioproductive fabrics.

To capture the problem of heterogeneity in the clusters, we have constructed a simple typology that seeks to differentiate the dynamic establishments from the nondynamic. Dynamism has been defined by the simultaneous existence of the use of formal accounting and a place of work separate from the house. Thus, on the one hand, business rationales have been incorporated, and on the other, subsistence rationales, linked to the household, have been separated from those of the business. Those units that do not meet these two conditions have been classified as nondynamic.[5] In this regard, the contrasts between the clusters are clear-cut: while in La Fortuna, three-quarters (75.5 percent) of the establishments meet the two criteria, this percentage is minimal (8.3 percent) in La Palma, with San Pedro Sacatepéquez in between (18.0 percent) but much closer to the Salvadoran universe. Thus, the economic fabric shows a certain level of heterogeneity.

In this sense, it is important to explore what factors are associated with heterogeneity. Table 3.2 compares, by cluster, the profiles of the establishments that are dynamic versus those that are not.[6]

The dimension that reflects the greatest level of differentiation appears to be the size of the establishment according to the number of employees. In fact, this is an indicator of accumulation, confirming that the dimensions selected in defining dynamism are analytically pertinent. In other words, those establishments with business rationales and investment capacity are those that show a logic of accumulation. Additionally, this is a dimension that establishes differences among the three clusters and that, therefore, appears to be universal. The same can be said,

Table 3.2.   Establishment Dynamism Profiles by Locale

Dimensions	La Fortuna (n = 49)		La Palma (n = 48)		San Pedro Sacatepéquez (n = 50)	
	Dynamic	Nondynamic	Dynamic	Nondynamic	Dynamic	Nondynamic
Women (%)	48.6	33.3	25.0	31.8	0.0	0.0
Age (average in years)	37.1	37.0	39.8	37.8	37.7	39.1
Educational level (average in years)	10.3	8.8	9.0	7.1	10.6	7.2
Experience (average in years)	7.5	7.7	20.0	14.0	16.6	17.5
Number of employees (average)	5.4	1.2	35.0	8.9	31.0	11.6

Source: FLACSO survey.

although perhaps not as strongly due to the Salvadoran case, with regard to education. Thus, formal human capital and accumulation of economic capital appear to be two generalizable traits of dynamism. The first of these refers to an inherent trait of the owner, while the second is a characteristic of the establishment. This combination confirms the nature of self-employment that continues to mark the majority of the economic units of these clusters. But a few particularities need to be highlighted. In La Fortuna, women have access to ownership of dynamic establishments, thus questioning a tendency of the past informality that while women had access to this occupational space, they were relegated to subsistence activities and not accumulative ones (Pérez Sáinz and Menjívar Larín 1994). However, this continues to persist in La Palma.[7] In the Salvadoran case, attention must be called to the association between experience in the trade and dynamism, which implies that, in this context, economic success has deep roots in time.

Thus, we have clusters that cannot be viewed as homogeneous and that entail diverse factors associated with heterogeneity. However, this analysis is just an initial approximation of this problem since, in the following chapter, we will delve deeper into the diversity of the socioproductive fabrics and modes of market insertion.

The existence of heterogeneity questions a central characteristic of the clusters: its cohesion. This characteristic is important since it has to do with whether only a few firms, the most efficient and competitive, are able to enter the global market or whether this integration involves the entire cluster because efficiency and competitiveness are socialized. In this regard, the issue of cohesion presents the problem of equity transcending households and expressing itself in terms of firms as well. Cohesion involves questioning whether we are faced with something more than just a group of establishments located in the same territory carrying out the same activity. This means looking into whether the territory can be preceded by the prefix *socio-* and whether *sector* implies something more than dedicating oneself to the same type of good or service. Let's start with the latter point.

In addressing the cohesion of the cluster, from a sectoral perspective, we need to refer to the phenomenon of external economies that, in Alfred Marshall's original conception, do not depend on internal factors of the firm but rather the general development of the sector in question, and thus offer benefits to the entire cluster. For the type of realities that concern us, we are talking about various phenomena, including the existence of a local labor market where labor can circulate without difficulty from one establishment to another. The possibility that the cluster has acquired a certain reputation in carrying out the respective activity is, in principle, something favorable for all the economic units. The dissemination of information about the possibilities of markets or obtaining inputs would be another relevant example of an external economy for the type of universe analyzed. In more analytical terms, and being true to the Marshallian origin of the term, three types of external economies can be spoken of: those of specialization, resulting in a division of labor between productive businesses and those dedicated to complimentary processes; those of information and communication that minimize transaction costs; and those of labor, as a product of the availability of a pool of qualified labor (Zeitlin 1993). In this sense, the problem of cohesion of a cluster involves two aspects. The first involves the presence of different types of external economies: the more there are, the more cohesive the cluster, and vice versa. Second, cohesion is synonymous with the degree of incidence of external economies: the more generalized they are, in the sense that they (external economies) benefit more establishments, the greater the cohesion, and vice versa.

The labor economies are more easily perceived in each of the clusters due to their high level of generalization. Thus, local labor markets exist with a labor force that is not only in sufficient supply but also adequate for the activities in question. The territoriality of this market is not limited to only the community but acquires a microregional dimension in the case of San Pedro Sacatepéquez, where labor comes from neighboring villages (San Raimundo, Santo Domingo Xenacoj, or San Juan Sacatepéquez[8]). But this projection is transnational in the case of La Fortuna where Nicaraguan labor is found.[9] Within this group of labor-external economies, collective learning can also be considered. This is evident in the case of San Pedro Sacatepéquez and La Palma, where the trade is learned in workshops, normally family ones, before becoming independent. Regarding this, it is important to remember, as was mentioned in chapter 2, the role played by the person who started the manufacturing revolution in San Pedro Sacatepéquez, whose workshop became a true training center for apprentices and the first producers in this locale. The cooperative la Semilla de Dios in La Palma played a similar role. These types of mechanisms are important for small establishments since, contrary to large businesses, internal resources cannot be mobilized to develop know-how (Helmsing 2001).

The external economy of the image of the cluster, also easily perceived and generalized, was not contemplated in the preceding classification. In the case of La Fortuna, this is associated with its selective advantage of being near the Arenal volcano, one of the principal tourist destinations in Costa Rica. San Pedro Sacatepéquez has acquired a reputation as a hardworking community where maquilas in the capital look for subcontracting work. In this sense, it is interesting to mention that the person mentioned in the second chapter as a maquila subcontract facilitator pointed out that, "we realized that we could not sell a contract without first selling the town, showing the contractors that San Pedro was an industrious town and not just a group. In 1987 we started this, selling San Pedro as an industry. Just imagine—there were eleven thousand sewing machines, a small Taiwan. You knocked on a door and found three or four sewing machines." And the handicrafts of La Palma have become the emblem of Salvadoran handicrafts. This last case is interesting since in meshing the local with the national, the image can be appropriated outside the cluster. In other words, this externality transcends the territory of the cluster, generating problems of nonlocal imitations, as we will see in the next section. But in general, it can be said that the cluster, and in fact the community, acquire a certain reputation recognized in the global market, offering benefits to all establishments in the respective cluster. In this sense, we face an external economy that operates in all three of the clusters under consideration.

Equally recognizable for its absence is the first type of external economy: that of specialization. Neither in La Palma nor in San Pedro Sacatepéquez can it be said that there has been a development of services and complementary activities to that of the industry. There are clusters with an undeveloped division of labor among establishments. This absence is a source for perverse economic dynamics, especially in the case of La Palma, analyzed in the next section. In terms of La Fortuna, the difference comes from tourist activity, with its plurality of activities (lodging, transportation, food, excursions, etc.). This fact inherently incorporates a certain division of labor between establishments, thus affirming that in this cluster, this sort of external economy exists.

Finally, it is important to delve into the economies of information and communication because they allow for illustrating the argument that externalities are not appropriated in an indiscriminate manner within the cluster. We have focused on the existence and availability of information about raw material providers and/or clients. This external economy is practically universalized in La Fortuna (91.8 percent of the cases), fairly generalized in La Palma (56.3 percent of the establishments), but limited in San Pedro Sacatepéquez (36.0 percent of the economic units). To explain, at least partially, these differences, it is pertinent to relate the circulation of information with the problem of dynamism of the establishments contemplated in the previous paragraphs. In this sense, for those cases considered dynamic, these percentages rise in the three clusters: 97.3 percent in La Fortuna, 100.0 percent in La Palma, and 44.4 percent in San Pedro Sacatepéquez. These results indicate a certain association between the two phenomena and that the dynamic establishments are those that make more use of this type of external economy. The conclusion is that the heterogeneity of the socioproductive fabrics appears to filter, to a certain point, this type of external economy, showing that information does not flow without restrictions throughout the cluster.

These reflections on external economies are summarized in table 3.3. From this table, what is clear is that the tourist cluster of La Fortuna is more cohesive due to the greater level of different types of external economies that are more generalized in their incidence. The difference is established by the universalization of the informational flows concerning providers and/or clients and, more important, the division of labor between establishments through the tourist activity. It is only in the case of collective learning that La Fortuna is at a disadvantage. The comparison between the other two clusters is not so clear. While in La Palma there is a higher level of informational flows, this cluster has problems with the national nature of its reputation. The appropriation of the local by the national makes possible nonlocal imitations, as we will see in the next section. Plus, in the case of San Pedro Sacatepéquez, the circulation of labor benefits a broader territorial market than in the Salvadoran case. But in both clusters, the great deficit in terms of sectoral cohesion is the lack of a division of labor among the establishments.

The issue of cohesion can be further analyzed by taking into account dimensions other than external economies in the clusters This is what has been attempted with the concept of collective efficiency (Schmitz 1995, 1999).[10] This proposal, in addition to recouping Marshall's analysis concerning external economies, incorporates two additional dimensions: cooperation among establishments and corporate association. Both constitute what, from this focus, has been denominated as joint action. In this sense, collective efficiency of the cluster includes a passive dimension, external economies; and an active one, joint action.

The virtue of this proposal is to project the issue of cohesion of a cluster beyond strictly the economic dynamics incorporating a new social dimension, with that of interfirm cooperation,[11] and policies, with corporate association. However, in our opinion, this effort is insufficient since it does not fully capture either sociocultural rationales or political-institutional ones that impact the cluster when the analytical reference point continues to be the cluster and not the community. In this regard, we consider that the concept of community capital and institutional thickness, respectively, have greater heuristic power.

This later concept, which will be discussed in the third section of this chapter, calls forth collective action emanating from the cluster in the institutional interworkings of the locale. If the owners of the establishments in the cluster are the same central actors of local life, probably the analysis of their organizations will allow for an adequate understanding of the

Table 3.3. External Economies by Locale

Type of External Economy	La Fortuna	La Palma	San Pedro Sacatepéquez
Specialization	Plurality of tourist activities	Minimal	Minimal
Information and communication	Universalized with more use among dynamic establishments	Generalized with more use among dynamic establishments	Limited with more use among dynamic establishments
Labor	Generalized circulation of labor with presence of Nicaraguan migrants	Generalized circulation of labor	Generalized circulation of labor extending into microregion
Symbolic	Arenal volcano as tourist destination	National symbol of handicrafts	Hard-working community

Source: FLACSO case studies.

political-institutional dimension. But this does not always take place, and it is to be expected that the institutional field is the result of differing types of collective actions, many of which have nothing to do with the cluster. In this more common situation, the concept of institutional thickness is more helpful.[12] In fact, from a focus of collective efficiency, it has been recognized that to respond to the challenges of globalization, joint action is not enough and broader issues of local governance need to be discussed (Schmitz and Navdi 1999). However, it must be pointed out that the term *governance* tends to apply only to the cluster and not the community as a whole as we propose.

Regarding community capital, this is a concept that incorporates cooperation but goes much farther in the understanding of sociocultural factors that impact economic behavior. Cooperation for collective production is the tip of the iceberg that is sometimes submerged. In fact, it can be said that this focus, in terms of collective efficiency, tends to privilege the sectoral dimension of the cluster, losing in a certain way its other dimension: territory. Helmsing (2001) has argued that joint action generates external economies in specific collective services provided in a nonmercantile manner, thus emphasizing the sectoral dimension. But it is important to remember that this concept has its origins in the discussion on industrial districts where the first formulations emphasized rather the idea of socioterritory as a fundamental part of this phenomenon (Becattini 1992). Nonetheless, with regard to developing trust for generating cooperation, from the viewpoint of collective efficiency, it has been argued that while sociocultural factors are important for the emergence of trust, its impact diminishes with time since the development of the cluster brings about differentiation within the community and nonlocal actors acquire a more preponderant role (Humphrey and Schmitz 1998). This line of argument can be taken to the extreme of minimizing the importance of the socioterritory and reducing the problem of relationships between firms and the process of learning to the monitoring of small establishments under the coordination of large businesses, especially multinational ones.[13]

Thus, we could conclude that our reflection is limited to the initial stages of the development of the cluster where collective efficiency has not fully reached it heuristic potential. But we believe that there is something more in terms of differences in the analytical perspectives. The subject in the viewpoint of collective efficiency is the cluster and its development in the face of globalization. On the contrary, we are trying to analyze these challenges in terms of the community that territorially houses the cluster. Our concern goes beyond the identification of factors that impact a set of firms so that they can efficiently and competitively insert themselves in the global market. It is the community as a whole, its cohesion and development in the face of the threats and challenges presented by globalization, that concerns us.

CLUSTERS AND COMMUNITY CAPITAL

As mentioned in the introduction, this trajectory of research on Central American communities inserted in globalization has been influenced by the reflections carried out by Portes (Portes and Sensenbrenner 1993; Portes 1998; Portes and Landolt 2000) on the term *social capital*. His characterization of different modes of social capital (value introjection, reciprocity, bounded solidarity, and enforceable trust) have been useful analytical tools for the study of these communities. However, for this text, we have decided that it is not convenient to use this term, taking into consideration Lin's (2001)[14] proposal limiting the phenomenon of social capital to those resources embedded in networks and differentiating them from other resources such as values, norms, and so forth. According to this author, these elements make up part of what is called *collective capital*, which, in our type of context, can be called *community capital* in that the community is the collectivity in question. However, we distance ourselves from Lin's proposal of analytically differentiating collective capital (in our case, community) from social capital. We consider that this distinction is not pertinent in the type of context that we are delving into. In effect, the networks that interest us are materially sustained through the same territory and, in this regard, are a community resource just like values or norms. This does not imply that all sorts of networks in which a community can be involved are territorial in nature: for this type of situation, the analytical distinction made by Lin is more appropriate. But the reciprocity that interests us, the interrelationships of owners of establishments in the cluster, has an unequivocal base in the territory. In other words, in our proposal, reciprocity and the networks that develop from it are a type of community capital, and it is from this perspective that they should be analyzed. This position brings us back to the modes of social capital presented by Portes and Sensenbrenner but considered as community capital. This means that many of the most suggestive reflections by Portes on social capital are applicable in the case of community capital since both terms are very similar. Perhaps the main difference lies in the fields of application. Our use of community capital is more restrictive, limited to neighborhood communities where the territory is key.

In this sense, we understand *community capital* as a process of appropriation of different types of sociocultural resources from the community by owners of the establishments of the respective cluster, potentially producing cohesionary effects on the same. However, several points need to be made. These points have been made concerning social capital, but, as we have mentioned, they are perfectly applicable to community capital as well.

This first point is that, just as the reflection on social capital, this proposal regarding community capital fits within the perspective of economic sociology that has questioned, through the concept of embeddedness, the idea that the market is autonomous by postulating that personal relationships, and the networks that sustain them, impact actions, outcomes, and economic institutions (Granovetter 1985, 1990). In this regard, it is worthwhile to summarize the three basic propositions of economic sociology. The first is that economic action is a form of social action. This means reviving the Weberian idea of economic action emphasizing its fundamental elements: on the one hand, the individual takes into account in his or her behavior, the behavior of other actors; and on the other hand, economic action has a political meaning since the economy is a source of power. The second proposition is that social action takes place socially. In this case, the key element is the incidence of networks in economic behavior. Finally, social institutions are social constructions. This last point means understanding the institutions of the economic world, as well as other sorts, as realities that are not external or prior to social action but rather a product of it (Swedberg and Granovetter 1992). In this regard, and in terms of our discussion, we consider that economic behavior within the cluster and in the face of globalization is influenced by community-based sociocultural factors, in that they are manifestations of social action.

The second point is that the term *community capital* refers to the old idea found in the dawn of sociological thinking, and that has to do with the advantages (or disadvantages) that an individual has by belonging to a group.[15] In terms of our context, this implies that the individuals that are (dis)advantaged are the owners of the establishments in the cluster. This does not mean that only they can access community capital, but it is this economic actor that interests us in this text.

In addition, the group to which they belong is not the cluster but rather the community. Remember that the term *cluster* implies sectoral and socioterritorial affinity. In the previous section, we analyzed the advantages of sectoral affinity in terms of external economies, but these should not be considered, in a strict sense, an expression of community capital. The provision of a common good or service does not imply membership in a group in the sociological sense since, in principle, the affinity is mediated through the market, implying an abstraction of the atomized links and isolating actors that would not have a reference for collective belonging. Obviously these actors can associate and from this association gain advantages that could be interpreted in terms of community capital, but then this would no longer be an external economy. In other words, external economies are not manifestations of community capital, or vice versa, and both phenomena should be kept analytically separate. This is not the case with socioterritorial affinity, which unequivocally refers to community capital. It must be remembered that tradition as the first logic of the making up of the socioterritory is that which generates identity, reinforcing a sense of belonging to a certain territory. And while national and global modernization redefine this, in the majority of cases we face a deeply rooted logic. In any case, this is the situation of the three universes that we are considering.

Finally, the advantage of belonging to the group has to do with the cohesion of the cluster and accounts for how the topic of community capital has emerged in this analysis. In other words, community belonging has to do with advantages that are individual but also have repercussions in the cluster since they bring about collective effects in economic actions.

The third point is that community capital has to do with individual actions. Sociocultural resources are not per se community capital unless members of the community, who convert them into capital and thus produce benefits, can individually appropriate them. For our analytical purposes, the owners of the establishments in the cluster carry out this appropriation. These observations bring us back to the reflections of social capital. The popularity of this term cannot be forgotten, and thus its more common use is due to the emphasis on the collective. Concretely, social capital is an attribute of communities and nations and is synonymous with civicness. This is Putman's (1993) proposal in his well-cited study on the divergent historic destinies of Italy.[16] This viewpoint has been criticized for its circular logic and its tautological consequences in reasoning: social capital is simultaneously cause and effect. Civic communities develop civic actions, and noncivic communities develop noncivic actions (Portes 1998; Portes and Landolt 2000). This presents the problem of the relationship between the individual and the collective with regard to community capital. Our posture is that there is a permanent dialectic between these levels. Thus, the resources, by being communitarian, are collective in nature. Moreover, the benefits can also be collective by seeking the cohesion of the cluster. But the appropriation of the community resources to produce these effects, and bring about the constitution of community capital, is fundamentally the result of an individual action.[17] It is only in this way, through an individual, that it can be argued that economic relations are embedded, and this is the great heuristic potential of this concept.

The fourth point refers to the different types of sociocultural resources that are appropriated. As was mentioned at the beginning of this section, we have used the proposal of Portes and Sensenbrenner (1993) of different modes of social capital that are perfectly translatable to community capital. These authors proposed the existence of four modes. The first is defined as *value introjection* and is based on the Durkheimian analysis of the noncontractual elements of the contract, and on the moral nature of Weber's economic action, and refers to certain shared ethics in which economic behavior is guided by something other than the mere maximization of profits. The second form is called *reciprocity* and refers to actions where personal ends are sought but do not involve market transactions. The third, *bounded solidarity*, expresses the reaction of the community to outside hostility or threats. *Enforceable trust*, understood as the subordination of individual desires to collective expectations, is the fourth mode of social capital. This is the well-known Weberian distinction in economic exchanges between formal rationality of universal reach and substantive rationality that is particular in nature. It is this latter issue that sustains the fourth mode of social capital since it is the ends and expectations of the collectivity that orient individual behavior. This proposal enriches the original conception of embeddedness.

Finally, in regard to the effects, these can be cohesive or divisive. This issue of negative effects is also found in the reflection on social capital, questioning the moral value implicit in this term and underlying the vast majority of the analysis that use it. Normally, social capital is viewed as something positive and desirable and thus emerges as a talismanic term full of promises. To consider the possibility of disadvantages implies criticizing this viewpoint as being marked with a certain level of naiveté (Portes 1998). The consequence is that there can be negative social capital with costs for individuals. In this regard, Portes and Sensenbrenner (1993) have identified at least three types of effects of this sort that are completely applicable to our term of community capital.[18] The first has to do with the possible costs of community solidarity and excessive demands that can bring into question the social networks that they generate. A second negative effect relates to social restrictions in receiving outside cultural values that impede their use and therefore their positive effects. And third, and possibly that which generates the greatest cost, are the tendencies that seek to maintain cohesion and homogeneity in the group by suppressing individual achievement and social promotion. The group perceives this success as a threat to solidarity since it questions traditional networks that play a role of collectivizing risk. Furthermore, the group guarantees that there is no emulation, by impeding this sort of behavior through the existence of shared norms (Abraham and Platteau 2000).[19]

With these points considered, we can now begin to outline our analytical framework, returning to the definition of community capital mentioned at the beginning of this section. This framework has three elements. The first has to do with the community resources that are sociocultural in nature. These represent the sources of social community capital but are not capital per se, as this contradicts the argument that this phenomenon has to do with individual actions, since these resources are collective in nature. In other words, the spring should not be confused with the water that you drink from it. The second element is the individual action of appropriation of these resources. Third, there are the effects that, as we have already argued, are interpreted in terms of cohesion in the cluster. This proposal means understanding community capital as a process based on social action.

In table 3.4 we make the analytical distinction relating triads of terms that have to do with community resources, their individual appropriation, and the cohesionary effects: values/internalization/identity, reciprocity/trust/cooperation, solidarity/reaction/organization, and norms/moralization/innovation.

The first thing to mention from this table is that the sources of capital refer to the four resources typically found in these sorts of communities. There are shared values referring to a common history; reciprocity takes place since this is not an atomized world in which exchanges fundamentally take place through the market and its power of abstraction but rather direct contacts are facilitated through the concrete territory; links of solidarity among members of the community exist based on sharing certain common interests; and there are collectively accepted norms that guide behavior. These resources are present, in differing degrees, and it is difficult to speak of neighborhood community, as we have here, without these elements. At the same time, all of these resources can be individually appropriated: values can be internalized, reciprocity materializes through concrete nonmarket exchanges, solidarity develops in the face of external threats, and accepted norms guide individual behavior according to collective expectations. Obviously this appropriation can take place in many social fields, and this is what we understand

Table 3.4. Modes of Community Capital in Clusters of Small Establishments

Community Resources	Individual Appropriation	Cohesionary Effects
Values	Internalize	Identity
Reciprocity	Trust	Cooperation
Solidarity	React	Organization
Norms	Moralize	Innovation

to be community capital. But the manner of appropriation and, more important, the results that it produces in each community are specific to each field. Regarding this, it is important to remember that other factors are present, and these are not simply products of the gestation of community capital. In the following paragraphs, we examine each of these triads separately.

The first form of community capital involves sharing a series of values that guide local economic activity. Of these values, the ones that interest us are those that make possible the formation of community identity.[20] This possibility can materialize as a historic process, particularly if there has been a virtuous dialectic between the corresponding economic activity and the locale, and both terms become synonymous and thus are interchangeable (Pérez Sáinz 1999a).[21] But with globalization, if this symbolic external economy emerges, as previously mentioned, others (firms in the global chain and/or global consumers) may recognize this, thereby transcending the cluster and thus involving a recognition of the community. In this sort of situation, a recognized community identity in the global world has been constituted, as a result of the globalized activity. When this is associated with prestige, for those who carry out said activity within the locale, the key factor in terms of community capital is if this collective identity is internalized by these economic actors in order to consolidate the other internal transaction, that of identity formation. In other words, does the globalized activity represent an important milestone in the labor trajectories of the owners?[22] If this appropriation takes place, the identity of these actors is consolidated, and it can be postulated that robust economic identities[23] contribute to stronger cohesion in the cluster. Thus, our proposal on value introjection, as the first mode of community capital, has to do with the processes that make up identity.

Reciprocity can be appropriated through nonmercantile exchanges and manifested through networks among proprietors with different types of nonmonetary loans (raw materials, tools, labor, information, etc.). But what is crucial is the trust that is generated, represented as the individual appropriation of reciprocity as a community resource. Here we face a generalized situation of trust that combines two of the types of trust proposed by Zucker (1986): *characteristic based* and *process based*.[24] On the one hand, it can be said that belonging to a community makes possible the identification of trustworthy and untrustworthy proprietors, acting as a sort of filter for the selection of those that enter into networks and those that don't.[25] But the other type of filter—and this is what is particularly important—is that trust develops through the repetition of these nonmonetary exchanges, demonstrating that this is based more on past experiences than future expectations (Durston 1999). If there is enough repetition, with opportunities for foul play that have not been consummated (Luhman 1979), the result is cooperation among establishments. This reminds us that cooperation is a function not as much of the generalization of nonmercantile exchanges within the cluster as of their repetition. The thesis is that with more cooperation, there is more cohesion in the cluster, while the absence of the first leads to a fragmentation of the cluster. Obviously, other factors can promote this cooperation—for example, if the cluster fosters a certain natural division of work, as in the case of tourism, with its plurality of complementary activities. Here cooperation will be easier to develop.

The threats that can be reactivated, developing bounded solidarity are those that emerge from globalization. It is with respect to this third mode of community capital that globalization shows its particularly cruel face. All types of threats lead ultimately to exclusion from globalization. These noncommunity dangers present new issues related to risk beyond those already discussed in the previous chapter in regard to vulnerability of the households. But here we consider that it is more pertinent to understand this risk as a product of knowledge about the future as well as of consent of the aspirations of a certain group (Douglas and Wildavsky 1983), in this case of the proprietors of the cluster. In this sense, the risks induced by globalization involve a level of uncertainty due to the volatility of globalization. Consent depends precisely on the cohesion of the cluster. If this is cohesive, it will be possible to obtain consent, and thus a solution will be found, or a better understanding of the evolution of the global market in order to anticipate its volatility will develop. But, if cohesion is lacking, the situation will be more unfavorable for facing risk since these elements, knowledge and consent, become problematic and the solution is unknown.[26] The most important effect of solidarity induced by external threats is the development of a business organization among the owners of the establishments. In other words, the formation of a collective actor is a key element; we will address this in the coming section. This formation is synonymous with cohesion in the cluster, and the absence of this collective actor denotes disintegration. In fact, in this and the preceding paragraphs, we have an explanation of the proposal of joint action based on the concept of collective efficiency. What needs to be highlighted is that the concept of community capital allows us to explain the causation process and not merely establish whether it exists.

Finally, the acceptance of norms depends on the existence of informal means for effective rewards and punishments. This mode of community capital refers to the distinction between two types of morality, limited and generalized, established by Platteau (2000). The first is restricted to members of a community and discriminates against noncommunity agents. According to this author, based on observations of sub-Saharan tribal societies, this type of morality is a disincentive for accumulation and functions, in terms of our analytical framework, as negative community capital. Generalized morality involves, just as limited morality does, the existence of norms that take into account the interests of others leading to both positive reciprocity (you are nice to those who are nice to you) and negative reciprocity (you are mean to those who are mean to you). The difference between the types is that generalized morality projects this type of behavior onto external agents—in other words, people in general without regard to personal, familiar, or ethnic relationships. According to Platteau, this type of morality allows for the development of anonymous exchanges and thus the constitution and development of the market. In terms of our analytical point of reference, the globalized neighborhood community, several points need to be made. First, the global insertion implies that generalized morality operates; otherwise this insertion would not be possible. Second, the possibility of appropriation of norms by the owners in the cluster implies that limited morality can be reactivated. Third, this morality is not necessarily limited to economic dynamics. Rather, this is fundamental in determining the type of competition that develops: based on innovation or imitation. The first is associated with the existence of norms, while the second expresses a relaxing or overlooking of these. The fulfillment of these norms involves the generation of community capital in terms of the moralization of economic behaviors that, in this case, avoid the predatory effects of imitation and rather seek profit through innovation. In this regard, the thesis is that cohesive clusters function through innovation while those fragmented are based on imitation. This differentiation in terms of types of competition is important since, in the literature on industrial districts, virtuous dynamics based on the interaction between competition and cooperation were emphasized.[27] Finally, if this limited morality develops in this virtuous manner, there is no reason for it to enter into conflict with the generalized morality. On the contrary, competition based on innovation should bring about a more stable insertion in the global market, leading to greater acceptance of the generalized morality inherent in the same.

Based on these more general reflections, we move on to an analysis of our universes of study, considering each mode of community capital.

In terms of value introjection, the first thing to take into consideration is that this symbolic external economy has been found in each of the three universes, presenting the plausible hypothesis that the globalized activity is viewed positively and constitutes a source of prestige in each of the respective communities. A possible manifestation of these phenomena is evident in the owners' levels of satisfaction with their activity. The extremes are represented with La Fortuna, where almost all of the cases correspond to these levels, and La Palma, where this is the situation in a little less than three-quarters of the owners. Thus, there are clear indicators that being a proprietor in the cluster does not represent a social stigma but rather quite the opposite. But this extremely positive image is significantly redefined when considering whether the proprietor would continue the activity if other opportunities arose in which she or he could earn more money. Here we face head-on the internal transaction of identity and the willingness to continue in the activity or break away from it when faced with more economically beneficial possibilities. This disjuncture expresses the dialectic between the sociocultural environment and economic behavior—in other words, the embeddedness of the cluster where the predominance of sociocultural factors mean continuity, whereas a rupture involves fragility in the identity. Here it is important to point out that the number of cases drops, especially in the Guatemalan universe, where barely one-fourth of the producers would be willing to continue with the activity. This is surprising since this is the universe with the longest trajectory in the activity and where it would be expected that identities would be more consolidated.

Combining both dimensions, satisfaction with desire for permanence, we find a clear contrast between La Fortuna and the other two universes. In the Costa Rican case, a little more than two-thirds of the owners are not only satisfied but also hope to remain in the business. In other words, it is a satisfaction that resists economic temptation and reflects a consolidated identity in terms of the internal transaction, betting on continuity. The same cannot be said in the other two cases, where barely a little more (La Palma) or a little less (San Pedro Sacatepéquez) than a third of the owners manifest this attitude of continuity. In this regard, it is important to uncover some factors that may be negatively impacting the processes of identity that are eroding community capital.

In neither of these two cases can we detect an association between the dimensions of the establishment used in the previous section and continuity or rupture. Nor is there a relationship with the heterogeneity of the socioproductive fabric. In other words, the owners of dynamic establishments are not more predisposed toward continuity. Instead, this differentiation is evident the case of La Fortuna, where it would appear that economic success is an important part of the identity process. Thus, it appears that we will have to look to factors outside the cluster such as the type of insertion in the market, especially in the globalized market.[28] In the case of La Palma, owners who directly export without intermediation to the global market appear to be positively associated with the internal transaction of the identity process. Thus, there appears to be a virtuous interaction between globalization and economic identity, suggesting that the establishments that export are the ones that benefit from this symbolic external economy, implying that these proprietors are more able to internalize this reprocessed image of the community. However, this cannot be generalized since this is not the case in San Pedro Sacatepéquez, as we will see in a moment.

In the Guatemalan case, the insertion into the global market takes place through subcontracting, regarding which a few pertinent points need to be made as related to the analysis of identity. In the first place, stability in the subcontracting nexus is relevant since this could generate insecurity and thus attitudes that are more likely to lead to a rupture in identity. What is interesting is that barely one-third of the owners consider that the business that has subcontracted them would abandon them if circumstances changed. In this sense, it is important to point out that security is generalized in the owners with an attitude of continuity, while in the other group, a quarter of the cases are unsure. On the contrary, two-thirds of the producers would abandon the nexus, showing no differences between the two groups. Thus, the fragility of the link is found rather on the side of the subcontractees and not the subcontractors. Thus, subcontracting is a source of dissatisfaction, but due to factors that are related to the San Pedran producers.

The crucial issue is that the level of breakage of identity exists in two-thirds of the cases when all of the work is subcontracted. But when the producer maintains some of his own production, more than a half of the cases demonstrate consolidated satisfaction. This finding allows us to outline a possible explanation. We think that subcontracting has eroded the identity that was founded with the insertion of San Pedrans into the modernizing process. As we mentioned in the first chapter, this identity was initially one of merchants that was maintained despite the conversion to production. San Pedrans used to travel on weekends, throughout Guatemala and even to border areas of El Salvador and Honduras, selling their products. The sale of this clothing, made during the week, tended to represent a social recognition of their work and thus constituted an important act of identity recreation. Subcontracting broke this direct link with the market and has eroded the identity formed over decades. Obviously there are cases that contradict this explanation in two ways: successful subcontractees that are clearly satisfied, and merchants in a precarious situation who are unsatisfied. But in general terms, we consider that this explanation is plausible. Thus, globalization through subcontracting has eroded community capital accumulated over decades, generating the opposite of the situation found in the Salvadoran case.

Young woman painting crosses at Semilla de Dios cooperative in La Palma. All painting tables are located near windows with good light. Each bottle on the table contains a different color of lead-free paint used in the intricate handmade designs.
Photo courtesy of Katharine Andrade-Eekhoff.

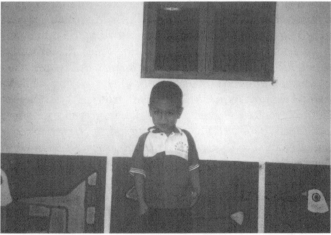

Five-year-old son of one of the cooperative members of Semilla de Dios, standing in front of the store and workshop in La Palma, Chalatenango, in northern El Salvador. Many of the women members of the cooperative combine their work and family responsibilites in flexible arrangements with the cooperative, generally painting products at home. The front of the store has been recently redesigned and includes brightly painted artwork on the outside and inside walls.
Photo courtesy of Katharine Andrade-Eekhoff.

Carpenter at the Semilla de Dios cooperative in La Palma sawing individual letters of the alphabet that will later be decorated. The cooperative is the only workshop that owns forestland for supplying some of the pinewood used as one of the main raw materials in this trade. It also owns a variety of electric saws and sanding machines used for cutting and preparing "blank" pieces of wood. Only men are involved in carpentry activities.

Photo courtesy of Katharine Andrade-Eekhoff.

Woman from La Palma varnishing a wooden hand-painted cross at the Semilla de Dios workshop. The shape of the brightly painted designs on the crosses is considered natural as opposed to the original design style, which is more geometrical.

Photo courtesy of Katharine Andrade-Eekhoff.

As argued, reciprocity manifests itself through networks. In our case, this has to do with a series of loans of different types of resources among establishments. These can be human (labor), material (raw materials, tools, etc.), or informational (information about suppliers and/or clients) resources.[29] These exchanges are broadly found in the three universes. Again, La Fortuna is the case where nearly all the proprietors have recently received[30] some sort of nonmonetary loan, while in the other two universes, about two-thirds of the owners report loans of this type. Delving into the profile of the person involved in this type of nonmercantile transaction in each cluster, we find that in the Costa Rican universe, the establishments are newer, with more employees, and more dynamic. In the case of La Palma, men tend to use these sorts of networks more than women. Particularly important to highlight is the finding that of the cases without networks, all of the establishments are nondynamic. In the Guatemalan universe, practically the same thing happens as in the Salvadoran case, where there is an absence of networks linked to a lack of dynamism. Additionally, as in the Costa Rican case, those owners with more employees are more likely to be involved in these types of networks.[31] These profiles suggest, as a general hypothesis, that there is an association between the absence of networks and the lack of dynamism in the establishment.

However, the fundamental point, as we have argued, is that these nonmercantile exchanges are based on trust that is solid enough to generate cooperation. In this regard, cooperation is only generalized in La Fortuna, with a little more than half of the cases, while in the other two communities, this phenomenon takes place in barely a fourth and a fifth of the cases in La Palma and San Pedro Sacatepéquez, respectively. Obviously, what is analytically interesting is delving into whether there is an association between networks and cooperation in each of the universes. In the three cases, it is clear that without networks, cooperation is very difficult, but not necessarily the contrary. This last point means that networks can generate differing levels of trust that may or may not materialize in cooperation. The key factor seems to be the frequency of the exchanges since only when this is high is enough trust generated to allow for the leap to cooperation, as has been previously postulated. Additionally, it is important to keep in mind that negative experiences of cooperation can profoundly erode cooperation. Along with these general reflections, particularities can be emphasized, at least in two of the universes. In La Fortuna, it should not be forgotten that tourism, with its plurality of activities, offers a more likely context for cooperation among establishments. Additionally, in San Pedro Sacatepéquez, none of the dynamic establishments are involved in cooperative processes. In the same vein, those owners who obtained their subcontracts on their own are less likely to cooperate. It is not easy to explain this, even hypothetically. What can be pointed out is that, in the Guatemalan universe, it appears that the dynamics of economic success are strongly linked to individualism.

In terms of bounded solidarity, it does not appear to be of any relevance in San Pedro Sacatepéquez. Although there have been attempts to replicate in other indigenous communities the success of this locale, the same type of development has not been obtained; this shows that certain processes are the fruit of very endogenous developments and cannot be externally induced. In this regard, the San Pedran producers do not fear the loss of their maquila subcontracts. However, a threat is beginning to emerge on the horizon: the need to overcome an insertion in the global market based solely on assembly work (this topic is analyzed in greater detail in the next chapter). However, this threat is not broadly perceived in the cluster and thus does not appear to be generating this mode of community capital.

Neither are external threats perceived in La Fortuna. The majority considers their locale to have a competitive advantage (the Arenal volcano and its environs) that is unique. But, as in the case of San Pedro Sacatepéquez, a potential threat that must be pointed out has to do with foreigners buying up land and rumors of the establishment of a large hotel chain that operates in Costa Rica. But there is no generalized perception of this danger among the owners in La Fortuna, probably because there already exists in the locale a large hotel (the Tabacón Hotel) with which there has been a beneficial coexistence. One of the smaller hotel owners points out:

> Tabacón even though it is a large business, benefits us a lot. The people that come to La Fortuna do not all fit in Tabacón. . . . The hotel does not have very many rooms, there are only about forty, so they bring their people, from the Presidente Hotel to Tabacón. They know that Tabacón doesn't have room. They place people in the Hotel Villa Fortuna, the Hotel San Bosco, the Hotel Las Colinas. They place people all over the place, and Tabacón supports the development of tourism in La Fortuna.

However, in the next chapter, when we look at the issues related to diverse insertions with international tourist flows, this opinion will be moderated, and it is one that we consider to be far too optimistic.

The situation in La Palma is quite different. In the Salvadoran universe, a third of the artisans perceive external threats that are well founded since their type of handicraft is being made in other parts of the country. What has been argued in terms of external economies, of a symbolic nature and of national projection, means that the type of handicraft can be appropriated outside the community. This does in fact take place in other communities in Chalatenango, the department in which La Palma is situated, and in other parts of the country that produce the same type of handicrafts. Additionally, referring to bounded solidarity, years ago an incident took place in which an external threat emerged when a North American client threatened to open a factory in Honduras due to the lateness of delivering orders. This brought the artisans of La Palma together; they activated their bounded solidarity to confront the threat by attempting to patent their designs in order to protect them. But, once the threat dissipated, organizational efforts did not emerge, but rather, ironically, negative effects with the copying of designs among the artisans in this community took place. This result presents the problems of competition between the artisans that will be addressed later. But we may conclude that these external threats have not generated sufficient responses to permit business organizations to materialize. As we will see in the next section, there are various handicraft cooperatives but without enough collective action in the whole of the cluster.

The last form of community capital refers to the moralization of economic behavior related to competition. Again, this does not appear to be a relevant issue in San Pedro Sacatepéquez in that subcontracting does not imply original designs, and thus there is no need to exercise social control so that competition is not based on imitation. Neither does it appear in obtaining contacts for subcontracting. In the case of La Fortuna, because the activity is related to personal services, imitation has limits. Obviously, there is the possibility of copying the way services are provided but the component of personal services is inherent in this activity and nontransferable. Additionally, in the case under consideration, imitation does not have negative effects, probably because there is sufficient demand. In fact, the vast majority of owners argue that their relations with other proprietors are collaborative (which does not necessarily mean cooperative) and not competitive.

It is in La Palma, due to the type of activity carried out, that the problem of competition and its modes is more clearly evident. Supposedly, the vast majority of artisans are sensitive to comments made by the rest of the community about their economic behavior. This implies the existence of a certain level of social control as related to economic activity and should translate into a moralization of the same. However, more than two-thirds of the producers complain about the competition of other producers in the same community. This problem is not as acute among the producers who export their products. As one artisan pointed out, "The markets are defined. Each workshop has its clientele in the international market. On a national level there is a lot of competition based on prices, and there are copies and little innovation." However, there are agreements regarding not copying designs among members of one cooperative. According to the member of this particular cooperative, "There is a lot of competition between producers based on prices, quality, and clients. In terms of copying, designs cannot be patented because if you change the color or any little thing, it is no longer the same product. But among the members, designs are respected. There is an agreement among the partners not to copy new designs."

This is a typical problem of handicraft clusters where the possibility of establishing barriers to protect innovation is very limited. The same tends to happen in design that is easily appropriated. Then competition based on lowering prices follows, in which workshops reduce their costs by using nonremunerated family labor and/or by using the house as a place of work in order not to accrue certain expenses. In other words, the logic of subsistence prevails over that of accumulation based on entrepreneurial rationales, artificially lowering prices. The market is flooded with undervalued products, thus entering into a predatory spiral. Additionally, the predominance of subsistence rationales tends to lead to the aversion of risk and thus innovation, reinforcing attitudes of imitation. It is only through certain technological innovations that imitation can be avoided, at least for a while, and thus profits can be generated. But this is only a possibility for the most dynamic. So it is not strange that in three-quarters of these types of establishments, the owners are not threatened by the competition of other local producers. On the contrary, a similar proportion of those that feel threatened is found in the nondynamic establishments. In other words, in the Salvadoran case, dynamism appears to be the best barrier to overcoming imitation and generating a profit based on accumulation. In fact, the vanguard of those that are dynamic, the direct exporters, protect themselves from imitations, selling their products only in the foreign marketplace and thereby limiting the possibility that their designs are copied. However, this conclusion means that economic factors operate, and therefore community capital does not have any impact. In other words, the moralization of economic behavior in La Palma is fragile and does not induce dynamics of innovation in this cluster.

All of these observations are summarized in table 3.5, which synthesizes, by locale, the type of community capital that has developed as well as the effects that it has had on the cluster in terms of contributions to cohesion.

Reading the table by locale, we can see that in the case of La Fortuna, the first two modes of community capital are very generalized. The internalization of values appears to be sustained by economic success as a result of the dynamism of the cluster that enjoys a sufficiently broad demand of tourism. Trust is an important ally in the characteristics of tourism, whose plurality of naturally complementary activities makes cooperation appear to be "normal." The other two forms of community capital do not appear to have much relevance in this universe. External

Table 3.5. Modes of Community Capital by Locale

Modes of Community Capital	La Fortuna	La Palma	San Pedro Sacatepéquez
Internalize values for identity	Generalized, based on economic success	Limited to direct exporters	Eroded by subcontracting
Trust for cooperation	Generalized, assisted by complementary nature of tourist activities	Limited with absence of cooperation	Limited with absence of cooperation
React in the face of external threats for organization	No perception of external threats	Threats of competition in El Salvador with limited organizational advances	No perception of external threats
Moralization for innovation	Limited need due to type of activity and dynamism of cluster	Generalized imitation limited in the case of dynamic establishments	Not necessary due to subcontracting logics

Source: Case studies by FLACSO.

threats are not perceived, leading to no organized reaction by the Fortunans. Nor is there any need to moralize economic life in order to limit predatory behavior in terms of competition. The peculiarity of the personalization of services and generalized economic dynamism in the cluster mean that problems in terms of competition requiring this form of community capital are not perceived.

It is in La Palma where all the modes of community capital are more clearly seen, even though their development is somewhat limited. The internalization of values is partial and has relevance for those artisans who have been able to export directly. These appear to be the ones that are truly benefiting from the image of the handicraft community that La Palma has gained in the globalized market. The trust that exists is limited, demonstrating that without networks there is no cooperation but that their existence does not automatically guarantee the development of trust. External threats exist due to the once-trademark image of the community that upon acquiring a national dimension has been appropriated by other places in El Salvador. Several years ago an external threat did induce a reactive organizational dynamic, but when the threat did not come about, the results were counterproductive in terms of imitation. This phenomenon is generalized and shows that the moralization of economic behavior in this cluster is lacking. Only the dynamic establishments have been able to erect protective barriers, but this reflects the preeminence of economic factors over sociocultural ones.

Finally, San Pedro Sacatepéquez is similar to La Palma in terms of the development of trust. On the other hand, it shares with La Fortuna the lack of relevance of a reaction to external threats or the moralization of economic behavior in the face of competition. The most important issue in terms of community capital in this community is the erosion of identity that has been detected. Subcontracting is undermining the identity developed over decades, through commercialization and the supposed entry into modernity by the San Pedrans. This mode of mediated insertion in the global market has generated generalized discontent among producers who, if given the opportunity, would abandon the activity that launched this community into globalization.

In the three universes under consideration it does not appear that community capital in its diverse modes has developed very far. This means that its effects in terms of cohesion in the respective clusters are limited. La Fortuna is the case with the most development, especially in terms of consolidated identity and cooperation. In La Palma, the impact is limited in terms of identity, trust, and organization. Plus, in terms of competition, moralization has been insufficient since imitation clearly predominates over innovation. But it is in San Pedro Sacatepéquez where the cohesive effects are more limited, especially due to the erosion of one of the most important resources of this community, identity, induced by subcontracting and with potentially very divisive effects in the near future. In other words, the generation of community capital is not simple even in contexts like those considered where community sociocultural resources exist. This conclusion makes relative the talisman that this term has acquired as a resource of salvation, and it reminds us that its activation and mobilization depend on the will for social action.

ACTORS AND INSTITUTIONS

La Fortuna appears more likely than the other two universes to have collective actors since this community has demonstrated a more consolidated formation of identities. On the other hand, the perception of external threats can also lead to the crystallization of organizational forms. In this case, La Palma is the universe that stands out. Regarding the type of organization (cooperatives, microenterprise associations, etc.), we have information that is worth delving into.

First, the owners in La Fortuna have a higher rate of association, a little less than half, while these levels are lower in La Palma, with a little less than a quarter, and barely a little more than a tenth in San Pedro Sacatepéquez. With regard to this last case, it must be remembered that it is located in Guatemala where the aftermath of the civil war continues to affect the country, specifically generating fear and apathy toward organizing. The profiles of the organized proprietors vary by cluster. In the Costa Rican case, the most relevant characteristics are the high number of employees and the dynamism in the respective establishment. The Salvadoran universe is the one with a more complex profile: a person with a higher level of education and experience in the trade, owner of an establishment with more employees, and, most important, dynamic. In fact, all of the cases of dynamism belong to some type of organization. On the contrary, in San Pedro Sacatepéquez we find the opposite: not a single dynamic owner belongs to an organization. Also, the San Pedran producers who are more taken to organization are older in age and experience in the trade. Thus, among these profiles, there is no dimension that is generalized, and what stands out are separate traits in each universe.

What is important in these organizational expressions, which imply the existence of collective actors, is their interaction with other actors present in the locale. This moves our analysis beyond the cluster and enters into the political-institutional arena. To approach this topic, we believe the pertinent concept is that of institutional thickness as it has been elaborated in terms of the dialectic between the global and the local (Amin and Thrift 1993). This approach involves various steps.

First, there is an allusion to the presence of institutions, or the existence of enough institutions of differing types. However, the number of institutions is relative and depends on the needs of each community. Thus, it does not always mean that more institutions lead to more density, since there can be a redundancy in their actions, which brings us to the next point. Institutional thickness is a question not just of magnitude but also of interaction among the institutions present. As a corollary to this point, it suggests the emergence of local structures and/or coalitions of interests obtaining collective representation that dominate and establish norms for economic activity. Finally, a consciousness may develop that makes actors feel involved in a common project. In other words, institutional thickness seeks the collectivization and corporatization of economic life in the corresponding locale. This concept has a qualitative dimension that has to do with the type of institutions present, the nature of their interactions, and the local power processes that result. But it also implies a gradual and accumulative process, as suggested by the term *thickness*. This means moving from a sufficient number of institutions and their interaction to the conformation of coalitions and from there the formation of a local development project based on consensus.

This proposal can be linked to the type of reality that we are analyzing in the present text. The local development project built on consensus should center on the globalized activity that has formed in the cluster, leading to the formation of a collective actor involving the economic agents present in the cluster as key protagonists.[32] In general terms, this presents the importance given to business associations. Helmsing (2001) has argued this importance based on three factors. First, the loss of importance of the state, which is not compensated by the action of the market as initially postulated from the neoliberal viewpoint, has led to the growing importance of other actors, especially business organizations, for the provision of semipublic goods and club goods. In this sense, Doner and Schneider (2000) have emphasized the market-supporting activities, such as the promotion of property rights, infrastructure, and less-corrupt bureaucracies, as one of the two contributions of this type of organization to overall economic development and not just to the members' benefit.[33] Second, the provision of services by these associations means that they can better face changes in the global market and its competition; this refers to the notion of collective efficiency. Third, these organizations can also contribute to the development of collective learning through small businesses in this rapidly changing technological world.

In the type of universes that we are analyzing, the first and third of these reasons are not very critical. In the development of the clusters under consideration, the state has not been a central actor. By being activities that are inserted into buyer-driven global chains, as we will see in the next chapter, the issue of technological change is not as crucial. Rather, the second factor, referring to the changes in the market, is fundamental for these sorts of clusters and thus the importance of organization among the proprietors of the establishments.

Two types of community capital can support the development of collective action among small entrepreneurs. The first has to do with the internalization of community values leading to solid economic identities. In this regard, as we have argued, actors with robust identities should be more taken to collective action. In fact, a virtuous interaction can be expected among economic and territorial identities but with a projection beyond the individual. The second form of community capital is that related to the reaction to external threats with the possibility for the crystallization of organizational forms. It is for these two reasons that we have pointed out in the introduction of this chapter that the issue of community capital serves as a bridge between economic actions in the cluster and political-institutional ones.

In addition, the processes of institutional thickening should include the local government in the center of the dynamic. It has already been mentioned that throughout Latin America and as a result of structural adjustment, state decentralization of differing degrees and modes is taking place. The key resides in the fact that the decentralizing dynamic not be separate from the insertion of the respective cluster in the globalizing process. This convergence can be analyzed in terms of elective affinity (Doner and Hershberg 1999) and is fundamental in order to obtain sufficient institutional thickness in contexts such as those studied in this text. The issue of decentralization presents a series of questions concerning its impact and consequences on the flexible productive activities as related to globalization. Doner and Hershberg (1999) have formulated three questions, advancing their own answers.[34] The first concern has to do with whether political decentralization creates a more favorable context than centralized policies for inducing flexible production. Although the answer by these authors has an affirmative tone, they also emphasize that the greater the technological requirements and more onerous the provision of collective goods, the greater is the need for centralized intervention.

The second question turns the terms of the first question around and seeks to know whether productive dislocation generates favorable dynamics for political decentralization. The answer, although with limited empirical evidence, is affirmative since new local interests are generated with the possibilities for new demands and political coalitions on a local level.

Finally, these authors ask about the explanatory factors of decentralization, identifying several. The first has to do with the possibilities of immediate political benefits by national actors competing for power with other actors. Decentralization can also serve long-term political objectives, through the provision of collective goods that a centralized authority cannot guarantee. Finally, decentralization can be a useful instrument for implementing and controlling geographic and/or sectoral policies.

However, an important factor related to this affinity is the level of overlap between both territories. In other words, the socioterritory defined by the globalized activity should coincide as much as possible with the jurisdictional space of the local state. If this is not the case, problems can arise. On the one hand, globalization can include a territory larger than one municipality in which a microregion would be generated, which from the point of view of institutional thickness presents the challenge of coordination among different local authorities. But, on the other hand, the opposite can also happen: the municipal space is larger than that delimited by the economic activity. Here, the interests of the local state are important as well as whether they are compatible with the globalized cluster.

Based on these analytical propositions, we can review the empirical evidence from the universes of this study. In the case of La Fortuna, five phenomena may be highlighted. In the first place, the small business tourist association (AMITUFOR), which showed great vitality at first, is now barely alive. Thus, the image that we have projected in previous paragraphs of being the universe with the greatest level of organization needs to be revised.[35] Its aborted development is an example of the difficulties of organizing in the world of small businesses where association is permanently questioned due to atomization. However, in this case we think that the main reason lies within the economic dynamism of the locale, induced by the increase in tourism, which does not present the need to organize, at least at this time, since every proprietor can reach his or her goals in an individual manner. However, the Chamber of Tourism of the Northern Zone, a business association that also entered into crisis a few years ago, appears to be in a process of revitalization through La Fortuna. This fact shows that this locale is the one with a more developed degree of tourism in the northern region of Costa Rica, and it opens organizational possibilities in this universe.

The second interesting phenomenon is the presence of an institutionality oriented toward the protection of the environment. The Arenal Conservation Area, part of the Ministry of the Environment and Energy, plays a fundamental role in the sustainability of tourism activities.

Third, La Fortuna suffers from the strong centralism that characterizes the Costa Rican state. This means that while there is an important presence of governmental institutions, their local orientation is limited. This centralism has an immediate effect on a municipal level due to La Fortuna's condition as a district and not the cantón of this locale.[36] Informants complain that the services provided by the municipal authorities in San Carlos, located in Ciudad Quesada, leave much to be desired.

Fourth, in more general terms, we might say that the institutionality that has emerged in this locale responds more to the old agrarian vocation. It is not clear how this situation can be made functional to respond to the needs induced by globalization through tourism.

Finally, the response to these deficiencies leads us to consider the fifth phenomenon, which has to do with the protagonism of the respective development association (ADIF) that is very active in providing services and carrying out infrastructure projects not offered or provided by the municipal authorities in San Carlos. This association functions as a sort of communal business with its own income (Civic Festival levies and income generated from the Fortuna River Falls Ecological Reserve) in addition to a small subsidy from the central government. It is through this association that the little existing institutional interaction takes place in the locale. There are ecological actions with the Technical College[37] and the already mentioned Arenal Conservation Area. Activities are also conducted with the Agency of the Agrarian Sector to carry out the Farmers Fair.

Thus, while La Fortuna has a respectable number of institutions, these respond to the orientation around the previous agricultural history of the locale. Additionally, little interaction among institutions has been found.

San Pedro Sacatepéquez is without a doubt the community with the least developed institutionality. We understand this to be the result of two issues. On the one hand, the geographic proximity of this locale to the Guatemalan capital implies relatively easy access to national institutions. But there is one big inconvenience to this: the almost total absence of institutions in San Pedro Sacatepéquez. At the same time, the divisive dynamics of subcontracting among the San Pedran producers must also be mentioned. As has already been discussed, this dynamic tends to isolate producers, leading in many cases to a loss of identification with the activity since these links are considered to be volatile. Furthermore, as has already been shown, this universe has a greater level of heterogeneity in the respective cluster. Thus, differences among the smaller establishments, which are the vast majority, and the consolidated factories are clear and generate resentment in some cases. In this regard, it is important to mention some of the complaints concerning the development of the Villasa project.[38] Some of the producers point out that

> when this project came, it was said to be a community project, but there are always some who take advantage and monopolize. . . . But only a few entered in Villaexport, setting up a private partnership, and from then on not all the people were able to enter, just the ones that were capable of it. With the private partnership, they only worked among themselves and not on a

community level that did not interest them. That is why I think the community project failed . . . but if we want San Pedro to develop, that is not the road.

The different organizational attempts have ended, until now, in failure. The following testimony from one of the producers is very clarifying:

> Several years ago there was an idea to set up a branch of the business association of exporters. This was with the engineer Colóm. It was a great struggle, but in the end the concept of what was wanted was not understood. Fees were established, but a lot asked why, if it was not going to produce results. The lack of knowledge and clear vision—there are doubts, distrust that emerged because of this. Later with M. we wanted to work on an indigenous business network, He was named the vice president, but it did not work. When one is left by himself, you lose incentive to go on, and they want quick results. After that I retired.

To this institutional desert, it needs to be added that in the past, the municipal government has not shown the least bit of interest in apparel manufacturing, although changes are beginning to be perceived.[39] In fact, the new authorities are studying the possibility of creating an industrial park on municipal lands and looking into possible sources of financing.[40]

The situation in La Palma is very different. This locale raises four political-institutional issues that merit discussion.

The first is that this community has the most institutional development, with almost thirty institutions present, including international cooperation, such as a project of the Inter-American Development Bank (IDB) (discussed later).

Second, concentrating on institutionality related to handicrafts, currently three cooperatives exist along with a handicraft association.[41] La Semilla de Dios, created by Fernando Llort and friends, as mentioned in the first chapter, is without a doubt the most consolidated cooperative in La Palma dedicated to production and commercialization. Currently, there are approximately twenty-five partners/workers, none of whom are founders. One starts as a worker (currently there are between fifteen and eighteen workers who are not partners) and later can opt to become a partner. Ten percent of their wages are given to the cooperative. They export mainly to Canada, the United States, and Italy. They also have a twenty-two-hectare forest for harvesting wood, but it does not meet all of their needs for this raw material. All of the partners and workers are from La Palma, and the designs are carried out only in the workshop.

Artesanos Unidos (United Artisans) is an organizational effort founded in 1990 and promoted through the now defunct Handicraft Development

Program (PRODESAR) of the European Community. At the beginning it had thirteen members, but currently there are only six. They work individually and collaborate among themselves for commercialization through a common store, exhibiting their products. They temporarily associate when there are large orders to fill. PRODESAR offered credit (financing was not limited to the members of this cooperative) and various training workshops.

The La Palma cooperative is one of the newer organizations. It is made up of a group of artisans who collaborate mainly through sales. An effort of ProChalate, this group is mainly dedicated to fomenting exports. It started at the beginning of 1997, formally with eighteen members but currently numbering about thirty, with various applications for membership pending. There is a common store for displaying items for sale and a place to purchase paints. Members participate in fairs on national and international levels, and the vice president of the cooperative participated in a handicraft fair in Spain in 1998. Some of the members have collaborated in the competitiveness program coordinated through the national government. The majority of the original partners have been affiliated with the FMLN, and some are even demobilized ex-combatants. They received on behalf of ADEL (Local Development Association) 150,000 *colones* (approximately U.S.$17,150) for loans for the affiliates of the cooperative. One of their ideas is to set up a web page for their products, but they still need to obtain a computer and trained personnel to manage the Internet connection.

The Association of Artisans and Artists of La Palma (ASAL Palma) represents a collective effort that cannot really be considered a cooperative. The group is composed of artisans and artists (some of the first in the community) concerned about the environment. They work with FIAES (Fund of the Initiative for the Americas in El Salvador) in a reforestation project. In the last several months, they have established links with other organizations of producers such as the coffee cooperative CoPalma and Las Pilas, which produces organic vegetables. The president of ASAL Palma is the wife of the former mayor under the ARENA party.[42] In addition to these local groups, the Salvadoran Chamber of Artisans (CASART),[43] Casa de las Artesanías, and EXPORSAL (promoting handicraft exports) also are present in the community. In other words, it appears initially that organizational efforts are well developed.

The third institutional phenomenon to point out is the role played by the city council. This group has been absent despite the fact that recent mayors are also artisans, but it can be explained in light of the partisan politics that characterize Salvadoran political life.[44] The strong national opposition between ARENA and the FMLN is reproduced in this municipality, which was a scenario of violent confrontations during the war. In fact, these differences are projected onto the handicraft organizations, around which some tend to organize based on political criteria. In other words, the associative development is relative due to these partisan politics.

Finally, La Palma experiences certain processes of institutional interaction. First, there are the actions in the agrarian area, which take place in two directions. There are those that have to do with the environment and that function in the department of Chalatenango to which La Palma belongs. And there are the actions carried out by ProCafé (an business sector institution for supporting coffee producers), along with ProChalate and CENTA, both part of the Ministry of Agriculture. Second, handicrafts along with tourism are an area of interaction where various institutions participate: the previously mentioned CASART (which offers technical assistance and training), Casa de las Artesanías, and EXPORSAL, as well as PROESA, a nonlocal institution supporting tourism activities. This initiative is being financed by the IDB. A series of meetings have been held to explain the nature of the project, in which owners of hotels, restaurants, artisans, cooperative leaders, and representatives from other organizations in La Palma have participated. But what is important to point out in all of these experiences, in which a configuration of coalitions can be observed, is that the initiatives as well as leadership in these actions lie with nonlocal institutions.[45]

Thus, La Palma shows perhaps the most developed level of institutional thickness in the three universes, but the quality of the relations is relative due to two elements: partisan politics and the protagonism of nonlocal actors.

The information from this section is summarized in table 3.6 and brings us to several important conclusions.

First, differences in terms of association are found, and these are the best expression of collective action on behalf of the actors of the cluster. The reasons vary from locale to locale. In the Costa Rican case, taking into account the lack of activity of the microenterprise organization of tourism, two reasons explain the predominantly individualist actions. La Fortuna is familiar with the passive mode of citizenship formation serving as the foundation for the Costa Rican state as a result of the 1948 conflict in this country.[46] In other words, Costa Ricans have enjoyed rights, especially social ones, without having had to fight for them. In addition, the dynamism that has characterized the development of tourism in this locale has brought about a generalized perception of unlimited opportunities that can be taken advantage of in an individual manner, and therefore collective action is unnecessary. In San Pedro Sacatepéquez, the reason for the lack of association needs to be traced, in addition to the devastating aftermath in terms of fear and apathy of the extended war that Guatemala suffered, to the isolation that subcontracting appears to be generating. La

Table 3.6. Institutional Issues by Locale

Dimensions	La Fortuna	La Palma	San Pedro Sacatepéquez
Association by small businesses	In crisis	Several cooperatives	Never existed
Presence of other Institutions	Institutions linked to agrarian world	Numerous	Subsumed within institutionality of capital
Role of municipality/ mayor	District/centralism	Exposure to partisan party conflicts originating from civil conflict	First-time interest in cluster
Possible coalitions	Initiatives related to environment	Various initiatives but with nonlocal leadership	None

Source: Case studies by FLACSO.

Palma, on the contrary, demonstrates the development of association through cooperatives and handicraft business organizations.

Second, the municipal government can play different roles, but in all three cases it is very limited, suggesting an absence of interaction with the respective economic activity. This is for all practical purposes absent in La Fortuna due to its condition as a cantón and the strong centralist tradition of the Costa Rican state. It has not played a role at all in San Pedro Sacatepéquez, although there are indications of change. In La Palma, despite the fact that recent mayors have also been artisans, the city government has not had much impact.[47] Third, the location of the community counts. Thus, due to its proximity to the capital of Guatemala, San Pedro Sacatepéquez has had very little institutional development since this is subsumed by the institutions of the capital.

Fourth, political divisions can be key. The clearest example of this is the Salvadoran case in which, while having the highest level of institutional development of the three cases, the same is trapped due to the aftermath of the war, currently expressed through confrontations between the two main political parties of the country. In other words, differences in the national agenda do not permit consensus making on a local level.

Finally, the institutional interactions are limited in all three cases, and the formation of local coalitions does not appear on the horizon, much less the possibility of establishing a hegemonic project that brings together the community as a whole in the face of globalization.

With this view from the political-institutional field, we finish our analysis of the internal dynamics of the communities. In the previous chapter, we tried to develop the dimension of equity, emphasizing rationales of household interaction where, as was expected, labor plays a predominant role. It is precisely through the labor market that we can move into the local economy and more concretely into the cluster of globalized activities.

Here we have emphasized three issues. The first is that heterogeneity presents problems in the cohesion of the cluster. At the same time, this factor has two dimensions: a sectoral one emphasizing external economies, and a territorial one referring to the issue of community capital and its modes. Finally, we have moved the analysis into the political arena where institutional thickness has been highlighted. In this way we now have all the analytical elements to discuss how the communities insert into the globalization process in order to identify the risks and opportunities they face.

NOTES

1. The empirical evidence analyzed in this chapter comes from a study of the establishments in each of the clusters: forty-nine in La Fortuna, forty-eight in La

Palma, and fifty in San Pedro Sacatepéquez. For more information, consult the appendix.

2. Formal accounting includes the use of accounting notebooks or contracting the services of a professional accountant. Accounts kept in other ways such as in a notebook or mentally are considered informal.

3. Guatemalan business organization whose members are businesses dedicated to nontraditional export production.

4. In Latin America, this homogenizing view, and thus simplified reality, was postulated by Hernando de Soto, an author with a huge impact on the common sense of policymakers and even among the academic world. In addition to the methodological fallacies of this viewpoint (concerning this see Pérez Sáinz 1991), the central prophecy of the message was never fulfilled: neither did *Sendero Luminoso* take power, nor was there an informal "revolution." History laughed at this minor prophet, pulling Fujimori out of its hat.

5. These are not necessarily subsistence since they might meet one of the two criteria, resulting in an intermediate situation. But for this analysis, due to the few cases considered in each cluster, we have opted for a dichotomous classification.

6. The dimensions under consideration are the same as in the previous table with the obvious omission of the location of the establishment and the type of accounting since these are the variables that define dynamism.

7. In the case of San Pedro Sacatepéquez, the problem of gender exclusion, as has been mentioned, is more basic: women have no access to ownership of the establishments.

8. This case is interesting because San Juan Sacatepéquez, for decades, had been the dynamic pole of this microregion, and today, its inhabitants look for work in San Pedro Sacatepéquez, which has emerged as the new pole.

9. Remember the analysis carried out on labor markets in the previous chapter.

10. There is an extensive bibliography on this analytical proposal. The *World Development* journal, volume 27, number 9, contains perhaps the best selection of work from the most conspicuous authors (Schmitz himself, Nadvi, Rabelloti, Knorringa, etc.) from this interpretive current.

11. We would add that cooperation can generate rents called *relational* and that it is one of the multiple ways of obtaining rent in the current globalized world (Kaplinsky 2000).

12. These ideas will be taken up again in the third section.

13. This would be the situation with the focus of "learning by monitoring" (Sabel 1994). In Central America, this perspective has been used to interpret the formation of a cluster of milk products in Nicaragua (Pérez-Alemán 2000).

14. As far as we know, Lin has carried out the most ambitious theoretical formalization on this term, showing that this is possible given the delimitation of the term.

15. The same can be said of social capital, about which notable contemporary sociologists such as Bordieu (1980) and Coleman (1988) are the main authors responsible for this renewal. For an analysis of the genesis and multiple exceptions to this term, see Lin (2000).

16. Social capital has been appropriated by the World Bank in an attempt to generate a new post-Washington consensus, replacing the state versus market opposition (Fine, 1999).

17. For this reason, we are not very inclined to use the term *community social capital,* proposed by Durston (1999), since we consider that this refers to the sources and possible effects of community capital.

18. Since the effects that are of interest to us here are those that build cohesion, we do not take into account negative forms of community capital. Rather, it would be the absence of community capital that would imply a lack of cohesion in the cluster.

19. This phenomenon is extremely clear in the case of tribal societies (Platteau 2000).

20. This analytical path moves away from the original proposal of Portes and Sensenbrenner (1993), for whom these values should serve as controls and orient individual economic behavior. We consider that in contexts such as those we are analyzing and following from these authors, this form of capital (social for these authors and community for us) is not very different from the other mode: enforceable trust.

21. For example, in one of the communities analyzed over the last ten years, but not included as one of the three universes in this text, the name of the locale, Sarchi, is synonymous with handicrafts. In fact, this community was declared the cradle of Costa Rican handicrafts, generating a virtuous cycle of identity between the economy and the locale (Pérez Sáinz and Cordero 1994).

22. This differentiation follows the model proposed by Dubar (1991). This author proposes that there are two types of transactions in the formation of labor identities. The first is internal in nature and has to do with how the person evaluates his or her occupational situation in function of past experiences and future aspirations. This transaction is guided by the opposition between continuity or rupture. The second transaction is external in nature and has to do with the exposure of the internal transaction with the "other." In this case, the opposition takes place in terms of recognition or disregard.

23. At the same time, this identity can interact with other types of identities (gender, ethnicity, etc.) through virtuous or vicious dialectics (Pérez Sáinz 1999a).

24. There is a third called *institution based.*

25. The problem of trust, within the community as well as with noncommunity agents, presents the issue of different types of moralities, limited and universal, that we will discuss in the fourth mode of community capital.

26. Taking into account the dimensions of knowledge and consent, Douglas and Wildavsky (1983, diagram A) identify two additional situations. In the first, certainty and consent exist and the problem is technical and the solution is calculus. And in the second, when there is certainty but consent is lacking, the solution is imposition or discussion.

27. This interaction, apparently paradoxical, is possible if competition is based on innovation, and suggests that the effects can interact between the two, complementing each other. In addition to this possible virtuous circle between cooperation and innovation, there is the complementary potential of identity and organization. It is to be expected that actors with strong identities are those that would be more likely to favor collective action and thus be able to develop forms for collective organization.

28. This issue will be taken up in the next chapter following upon our methodological proposal of looking at the global from the local.

29. These last ones were used as an indicator of the external economy of information. Regardless, in that this communication flow takes place within the context of networks, it is also considered in community capital but in a differing analytical focus.

30. Reciprocity also involves lending, but we have limited this analysis to receiving since this is a more trustworthy view of the true impact of these sorts of networks.

31. In the Guatemalan case, we need to point out that in a third of the cases, the subcontract was obtained through networks. But the most recurring mode, for half of the establishments, has been their own initiative.

32. This means that in a given locale, institutional thickness can come about but without relating to the structured activity of the cluster. This would mean that there is a divorce between both elements with limited results for the insertion of the locale in the global market.

33. The other type of activity is market complementing, which includes different types of actions: concertedly contributing to the reduction of inflation, promoting labor skills, establishing quality standards, and others.

34. The empirical references of these authors are mainly in East Asia, but they also attempt to compare them with some Latin American experiences, especially in Mexico.

35. The reason is due to different points of time in gathering data. Around mid-1998, data were gathered on the establishments, while the institutional interviews were carried out a year and a half later.

36. In Costa Rica, *cantón* is synonymous with *municipality*, and it is composed of districts that are the most basic political-administrative unit.

37. This technical college offers a degree in tourism, but, as an informant mentioned, the professors, in order not to lose their jobs, which are focused on agricultural activities, discourage students in order to "make peons, peons, peons."

38. This is an organized group of producers who were able to establish the largest factory in the community. We refer to this project in the next chapter.

39. In the middle of 2000, we presented results from the study in the community. This activity was jointly organized with the municipality as an expression of the interest to try and get closer to the producers.

40. This initiative, potentially very important, will be taken up again in the next chapter when we identify the big challenges that each of the three locales face.

41. A fourth cooperative exists, Jesus Obrero Workshop, which started in the metropolitan area of San Salvador, in the municipality of Soyapango, as an initiative of former FMLN combatants. One of the members moved to La Palma with the idea of setting up a workshop. However, at the time of carrying out the fieldwork, it was not possible to locate them.

42. ARENA, or the National Republican Alliance, is the conservative political party that has dominated Salvadoran politics since the end of the 1980s.

43. This institution grew out of PRODESAR and incorporates artisans from all over the country. At the time the fieldwork was carried out, the president of CASART was one of the artisans from La Palma.

44. In a visit to the community at the end of 2002, we noticed that the current mayor and city council have begun to demonstrate a shift from previous periods.

While not necessarily directly involved in all the various initiatives to promote handicrafts in the community, the local government has clearly been engaged in facilitating contacts and activities of a wide variety between artisans and other local and nonlocal actors.

45. A further initiative that emerged following all the fieldwork has involved CONAMYPE, the central government institution that supports micro- and small enterprise development, establishing four handicraft centers in various communities in the country. One of these centers has been formed in La Palma and incorporates a store, a variety of courses and technical assistance for small business owners, and the use of the Internet. However, yet again, the impulse comes from nonlocal actors.

46. This was a short conflict that resolved the oligarchic domination in this country and resulted in a democratic solution, which was not the case in the other Central American countries. The result brought about a refounding of the country based on the development of a strong interventionist-oriented state, especially in terms of social policy.

47. As noted earlier, this may be changing in La Palma.

4

Globalization
and Community

This final chapter has three objectives. First, it seeks to project the analysis out of the community context by looking at how the activity that has structured the cluster is inserted into the global market. At the beginning of chapter 2, when we first introduced the universes from this study, we discovered that each community had entered through differing processes. Here we try to identify the current modes of insertion in globalization for each cluster, completing our interpretative panorama. This task will be carried out in the first section.

With all the elements, in the second section we will present a synthesized analysis of the three universes—our second objective. We highlight the main local dynamics by discussing information from the first section as well as the previous chapters. This exercise of synthesis incorporates the threats and challenges that global insertion presents in each community.

In the third section, we will present an integral analysis based on the dialectic between the local and the global in the type of contexts considered, focusing on a central concern of how to upgrade the entire community. As we have argued in the introduction, while our empirical points of reference are Central American communities, we believe that some characteristics can be generalized and applied in other locales. Thus, this attempt at generalization offers an analytical framework to understand the insertion of neighborhood communities with a cluster of economic activities in the current globalized world. This is the third objective of this chapter.

GLOBAL CHAINS AND UPGRADING OF THE CLUSTER

To analyze global market insertion, without a doubt, the analytical framework of global commodity chains is of great use since it offers an adequate understanding of how the global economy is structured and functions.

There are four elements to these chains:

- the production of value added through a group of economic activities;
- geographic dispersion of productive and commercial networks involving businesses of different types and sizes;
- the existence of a structure of power among firms that determines how different resources (human, material, financial, etc.) are distributed and allocated along the length of the chain; and
- the presence of institutional contexts that serve to identify conditions (local, national, or international) that make possible each moment of the chain.

These can be producer-driven or buyer-driven chains (Gereffi and Korzeniewicz 1994; Gereffi 1995; Gereffi and Hamilton 1996).[1] This distinction depends on the type of firm that controls the governance of the chain—in other words, who determines the parameters of what, how, when, and how much is produced (Humphrey and Schmitz 2001). If it is a production firm, this falls into the first type of chains; if is it a buyer firm, then the second. It is this latter case that is relevant for our cases of study and merits more specification.[2]

In the buyer-driven chains, commercial capital prevails; activities are concentrated in design and commercialization; economies of variety and scope serve as entry barriers; nondurable consumer goods such as clothing, shoes, and toys are produced; local firms dominate the final stages of production; networks are based on market linkages, and these tend to be horizontal (Gereffi 1995). The control of these chains is on the side of the buying firms, which are the ones with true market access. In this regard, it is worthwhile to summarize the changes that have operated in the market in the last several decades, especially in terms of competition, that largely explain the power of these types of businesses. A growing number of products have been exposed not only to price competition but mainly to differentiation and continual redesign. In other words, quality and volatility emerge as the new regulating principles of the market (Piore and Sabel 1984). This explains the need for governance from within the chain by the leading firms in order to manage risk in terms of quality and on-time delivery (Humphrey and Schmitz 2001).

In terms of the present market configuration, the emphasis on quality, questioning the typical indifferent mass production of the Fordist era, can be interpreted from the classic Marxist perspective: use value is back on the scene. Use value's main dimension is probably not so much material, the true utility of the good in question, but more symbolic in nature. It is in this sense that the trademark of a product plays a fundamental role; additionally, it allows the firm to captivate consumers when more choices are available in the market (Gereffi 2001). Thus, it is through differentiation in consumption that status is constructed. Consumers not only are willing to obtain the goods available in the market, as has been the case in past decades, but also through consumption aspire to new forms of social mobility (Cerny 1995). In this sense, Appadurai (1996) has argued that the consumer has been fetishized in that it has become a sign upsetting the centrality of social action that appears to correspond to consumption rather than production. Consumption appears as the motor force of capitalism, thus eclipsing production (Comaroff and Comaroff 2000) and changing the emphasis of the formation of identities from productive to consumption without the disappearance of class identities (Storper 2000). Thus, it should not appear strange that, along with firms (especially the multinationals), consumers have emerged as the actors within globalization, although their possibilities for protagonism are much more limited than those of firms.

The key issue for this type of chain as well as producer-driven ones is how to gain power in the chain. This brings us to the topic of upgrading, which incorporates various analytical elements. The first is in terms of product[3] and involves moving from the production of simple goods to more complex ones. The second involves moving from economic activities of assembly to original equipment manufacturing[4] and then to original brand manufacturing. Third, upgrading on an intrasectoral level implies increasing the forward and backward linkages in the chain.[5] Finally, upgrading on an intersectoral level implies moving from labor-intensive activities to those that are intensive in not only technology but also knowledge (Bair and Gereffi 1999). At the same time, upgrading is related to organizational learning, which in contexts such as ours refers to the accumulation of know-how through the direct business practice based on the very elements of the organization (routines or operating procedures, organizational structure, management of documents, etc.) more than on that generated through research and development activities. In other words, the foundation lies in the accumulation of know-how (including minor innovations, specializations and competencies, and implicit know-how that improves efficiency). It is this learning that makes upgrading of the firm in the chain possible, thereby reinforcing its position within the chain (Gereffi and Tam 1998).

The concept of upgrading is a useful departure point, but it has limitations for the contexts of neighborhood communities. For example, the concept has been used in terms of industrial production. Thus, its heuristic capacity needs to be broadened to agrarian activities and services.[6] As we will see, of our three universes, these analytical proposals can be applied without any problem in San Pedro Sacatepéquez because the respective cluster is dedicated to a manufacturing activity; but in the other two cases, we need to rediscuss the propositions. Also, the upgrading concept is limited to interfirm relations and the institutions that make viable its governance. On the contrary, the social dimension, and therefore the welfare of the population present in the corresponding socioterritory, is not explicitly considered. This is its greatest limitation, and, as we argued in the introduction, it reduces the possibility of considering the term *upgrading* as useful for rethinking development in the context of globalization. This limitation will be addressed in the third section of this chapter; for now let's look at the question of upgrading the cluster, analyzing first how the cluster integrates into the global market.

Let's review the insertion in the global market case by case. In La Fortuna, the activation of the Arenal volcano has led to this community becoming one of the main international tourist attractions in Costa Rica. La Palma, in the context of the civil war in the 1980s, was able to export its handicrafts, which have become a symbol of the country. And San Pedro Sacatepéquez became inserted in the global dynamic when maquila production increased in Guatemala and when legislative changes at the end of the 1980s allowed for subcontracting. But, as we saw in the previous chapter, the clusters of small businesses structured around the globalized activity are heterogeneous. This means that the insertion in the global market is differentiated and that there is not one single route but rather several in each of these universes.

In the case of La Fortuna, the first thing to point out is that almost all the small hotels report that their clients are foreign tourists. In other words, this is a cluster that is highly integrated into the global market. However, this insertion takes place through three means. The first is that which takes place through nonlocal agencies but includes establishments in La Fortuna, particularly tour operators that transport visitors from their hotels in the Metropolitan area or sometimes directly from the airport. Less than a fifth of the establishments obtain clients in this way. In this commercialization chain, obviously the nonlocal agent is the one that has control and thus keeps the majority of the profit, limiting local participation; additionally, visits tend to last only one day. Another type of arrangement is that which exists among larger hotels in the area and nonlocal travel agencies offering the possibility of a stop in the center of La

Fortuna for lunch. The restaurants that benefit depend on their good relations with the larger hotels. This is the case of the main hotel in the
area, El Tabacón; the testimony in the previous chapter positively viewed
the impact of this large establishment in the locale, but it should be
reevaluated since its effects are rather limited. Finally, direct commercialization takes place when tourists, by their own means, arrive in La
Fortuna seeking the necessary services. This is without a doubt the most
generalized mechanism. Plus, some of the small hotels have established
smaller chains with local tour operators. These operators leave publicity
material in the lodging establishments, and the proprietors of these receive a commission for each client provided to the operator. Obviously,
this sort of link is the one that leaves the most profit within the local
economy. The opposite extreme, in terms of economic impact on the local economy, is found through the first mode, while the second represents an intermediate situation with an impact concentrated in the larger
establishments.

In terms of La Palma, several different mechanisms for market insertion can be identified. The most direct involves direct sales through
stores that exist in La Palma. This town is located on one of the principal
thoroughfares to the Honduran border, which means that there is a
decent amount of traffic and travelers of differing sorts.[7] Direct sales includes selling products made by the owner but also products made by
other artisans, especially from smaller family workshops. The incidence
of this mode of sale is relatively small, with less than a tenth of artisans
marketing their products in this way.[8] There are also sales through intermediaries in the handicraft markets of San Salvador. This is the most generalized mode, with a half of the cases. The third mode is through
exports, mainly via intermediaries. Direct international sales are the final
form of insertion.

These latter two modes entail two issues to highlight. First, the products are of better quality (in terms of the wood used, process of drying,
nonleaded paint, packing of products, etc.), and orders are completed on
time. Second, fair trade networks have played a fundamental role in international commercialization of handicrafts in La Palma. The first of
these modes does not involve an insertion in globalization, strictly speaking, since the buyers are mainly national tourists as opposed to international, given that this community is located far from the capital and,
until recently, has not been easy to reach. (This situation may change in
the future if international tourism develops in the area.) Rather, it is other
modes of sales that integrate this handicraft cluster into the global market. The majority of buyers in the artisan markets in the capital are
clearly international tourists, and direct exports is obviously an insertion
in this market. With the exception of this last mechanism, nonlocal

intermediaries dominate the chain, and thus the profit that remains in the community is limited.

Four modes of insertion in the market have also been detected in San Pedro Sacatepéquez. The most generalized, submaquila, involves a contract with a company generally located in the metropolitan area that is the representative of a foreign firm, generally from the United States since this is the main destination for Guatemalan apparel exports. The San Pedran producer is limited to assembly of different pieces and does not cut the material, and auditing is carried out externally.

Submaquila also occurs when manufacturing plants in Guatemala are overwhelmed with an order that exceeds their productive capacity and seek out San Pedran producers to fill the order on time. The second mode is better than the first since it involves a direct contract with the foreign firm, and the San Pedran producer not only assembles the pieces but also carries out other operations. This sort of situation happens with the larger businesses and those that have a warehouse for materials and cutting, production, review, and packing rooms.

The third mode also refers to subcontracting but with national firms that are not inserted in the maquila regime. These export or sell in the Guatemalan market, competing with other imports. Here pirated trademarks can be found, a sui generis response to market openings induced through structural adjustment programs.

Finally, traditional production is targeted at the national market and border areas of Honduras and El Salvador; there are even cases where the San Pedran producers have established their own brand name. This final mechanism of insertion does not, strictly speaking, involve an insertion in the global market but is generally combined, as in the third situation, with the first mode. In other words, the vast majority of San Pedran producers are globalized although in differing degrees; in fact, less than a tenth of the producers contract out less than half of their production. Without a doubt the direct contract is the one that offers the most favorable insertion for local producers. Because of this, it is important to describe, if only briefly, the development of one of these experiences, that of Villasa, mentioned in the previous chapter.

This group organized through a contract with the Van Heusen firm in 1988 after a Turkish company did not fulfill their contract. The U.S. representative of the company in Guatemala, Alvaro Colóm, had a long history of contacts with the San Pedran producers, having previously sold them sewing machines. He proposed that the contract be carried out by a group in San Pedro Sacatepéquez, but the U.S. firm insisted on guarantees. Surprisingly, these were provided by the president of Guatemala at that time, Vinicio Cerezo, who had recently visited San Pedro Sacatepéquez and, as a good politician, promised assistance. With this unusual backing, Van Heusen could not refuse and thus began a relationship that has lasted until not long ago. In 1990, the Villasa company was founded; however, the partners did not close their own workshops. The first contracts were carried out under the first mode mentioned: subcontracts but purely assembly. But at the beginning of the 1990s, Van Heusen offered a low-interest loan to obtain more advanced technology. In this way, this group of producers became the ones with the most modern machinery at the time in the locale. This action demonstrated that the subcontracting firm wanted to establish lasting ties by bringing about technological innovation. Later, these ties developed into direct contracts. The new link was very beneficial for Villasa and allowed the company to build an industrial facility on the outskirts of the town, where at one point up to three hundred workers were producing about 1,500 dozen shirts a week exclusively for and directly exported to Van Heusen, whose headquarters in New York had an office dedicated to Villasa.

However, this idyllic relationship has recently ended. The explanation differs depending on the informant. The owners of Villasa argue that the U.S. firm simply left Guatemala. In reality, the company closed its plants due to union problems. Van Heusen has been the only business that recognized a union in the maquila sector in Guatemala. The rest of the maquila businesses focused their hostility on them due to the precedent that it established. Other San Pedran informants point to problems in the management of Villasa as the cause of the end of the relationship. Regardless, the local business is now working at a third of its capacity and has had to return to contracts under the mode of submaquila. In other words, it has suffered a real downgrading. This example perfectly illustrates the opportunities and risks of globalization.

The information on the different modes can be reinterpreted in terms of the basic issue of the chains: upgrading (see table 4.1). The upgrading typology has been thought of in terms of industrial production. Of our cases, only the Guatemalan universe fits into this analytical framework without any difficulty. The other two cases present problems that require more precision. For this reason, we propose a horizontal reading of the table in order to end with an interpretation by locale.[9]

In terms of the first type of upgrading, this needs to start by expanding the activities to include services. However, this type of activity presents difficulties when considering upgrading from simple to more complex services. Limiting ourselves to tourism and La Fortuna as the point of reference, lodging, which is of concern in this cluster, can be thought of in terms of simple/complex. Thus, it could be said that renting a room in a private home would be an example of the simplest, while a room in a hotel with multiple stars and all the additional

Table 4.1. Issues Related to Upgrading by Locale

Types of Upgrading	La Fortuna	La Palma	San Pedro Sacatepéquez
Product/services	Differentiated	Unique but without perspectives for redesign	Simple
Phases	Does not apply	Does not apply (pre-Taylorist with all phases)	Assembly (only sewing), but factories tend to have phases of cutting and finishing
Linkages	With local tour operators	Nonexistent	Nonexistent

Source: FLACSO study.

services (bar, pool, cable TV, etc.) would be an example of complex. But this sort of analysis means betting on a strategy of upgrading that implies that a certain type of service is ideal and desirable. However, it can be argued that there are tourists who don't look for a panoply of material services but are more interested in personal services and getting to know the place. In this way, small hotel establishments have better possibilities for offering this type of service as opposed to the larger hotel, where the treatment is unavoidably impersonal. Obviously the small scale implies that it is impossible to offer material services. Thus, the problem of upgrading in terms of simple/complex appears to be pertinent when the supply is indifferent but is diffuse when differentiation is sought.

La Fortuna offers mainly a differentiated service, although Tabacón, the large hotel, tends toward indifferentiation. But two important issues lie behind this discussion. The first is related to the models of tourism. Cordero (2000) has suggested three types in terms of a dialectic between the global and the local. The first is called *segregated* and represents an enclave situation where a nonlocal hotel complex imposes itself on the locale with passive community participation limited to the provision of labor. The opposite model is *integrated* and is the fruit of endogenous development from the community itself. La Fortuna would be closer to this type. Finally, there is the hybrid mode called *relatively integrated*. These models point toward different interactions between the local and the global in terms of grades of asymmetry. But there is also a discussion in terms of tourism as an appropriation of place that refers to the inclinations of the client. It should not be forgotten that tourism, in that it implies moving from the place of residence, involves questioning the place of the everyday. In this sense, the disjuncture is that of displacement versus what we could call the false trip. This last situation is psuedoabsenteeism in that what is pursued is minimizing the rupture with the place of residence. Options that imply the maximum of commodities and feelings of protection from the unknown are sought. This involves the consumption of the nonplace, the extreme expression of globalization where time dilutes space, as argued in chapter 1.[10] You can travel around the world in much less than eighty days, sleeping in the same type of bed or using the same type of towels, if you stay in one of the big international hotel chains. In contrast, opting for the unknown implies really traveling and confronting another space that represents a place that is distinct and questions the original. Here, the homogenizing logic of globalization is paradoxically shaken. The revolution in communication and transportation made possible by globalization also makes possible the discovery of these other places and more importantly, the discovery of "others." The world has become smaller, but at the same time there are more opportunities for discovering its diversity.

This type of upgrading also has other interpretive problems in the case of handicraft activities even though they are production and not services. Here the dichotomy of simple/complex also runs into problems since the product is defined more for its uniqueness. Handicrafts are not simple or complex but unique. It could be argued that there could be upgrading in terms of moving from a product generated from popular art to "cultured" art. In the case of La Palma, it needs to be remembered that the handicraft activity did not emerge as the fruit of a historic tradition in the community but was introduced by cultured artists, even though local artisans later appropriated it. But there is a certain possibility of refinement in the designs that allow for new niches to be opened, and in this sense there could be upgrading.[11] However, this process cannot be interpreted in terms of simple to complex. It does not involve a gradual process but rather a qualitative leap due to the unique nature of handicraft production. In the case of La Palma, the lack of innovation is reflected by the relative absence of the development of new designs.

The issue of design, fundamental in the handicraft activity, presents another type of discussion. This is related to a sort of intersectoral upgrading that is not presented in table 4.1 since it does not appear on the horizon of the three universes. But in this case, we could consider upgrading of this sort, still in the line of transformation of wood, if the production of goods with greater value added were to take place. Here we are thinking about furniture making that could be inspired in the already-existing handicraft tradition. But this possibility does not appear to be on the horizon in La Palma.

Where the interpretive proposal has no problems is in the case of San Pedro Sacatepéquez. All producers are dedicated to simple production that in the jargon of apparel manufacturing is known as *basic*. More complex levels of production known as *basic fashion* and *fashion* have not been detected in the community, although some businesses in Guatemala have developed this. As previously mentioned, only in the case of some producers for the local market have pieces been developed that are more complex than those demanded by subcontracting.

In the second type of upgrading, again there are problems in tourism. In that tourism implies a gamut of services that go beyond just lodging, upgrading would be synonymous with broadening this supply. But this broadening has economic limits. Transportation activities are a good example. Consider a small Fortuna hotel that has been able to establish direct communication, via the Internet or other means, with the client, who gets picked up at the airport by a hotel representative and taken to La Fortuna. This additional service would be an expression of upgrading, but this dynamic cannot go much farther. The next step would be international air transportation that is an insurmountable barrier due to the investment involved. But, even within the locale, it is not clear that expanding the activity to tours makes sense. Not even the large hotel chains have their own travel agencies. In other words, tourism suggests a plurality of activities that involves a certain division of labor among firms, which means horizontal cooperation as opposed to vertical integration. And this universe reflects this argument. In other words, there is no upgrading of phases because this makes no sense.

Handicrafts also present particularities for this type of upgrading. In this case, we are dealing with a pre-Taylorist organization of the labor process involving full integration of all the phases. There are no phases to recover through upgrading. This is different in the Guatemalan case, where we have seen two types of situations. The most generalized situation, referring to the typical cases of subcontracting, is where the activity is reduced to making or sewing pieces. But we have also seen how factories, through direct contracts, have been able to incorporate other phases and develop cutting/making/trimming. It needs to be pointed out that the appropriation of some of these phases, in particular cutting, implies infrastructure facilities that require ample room. We also cannot forget that the vast majority of San Pedran workshops can be found in the workers' own houses with the consequent limitations of space. In other words, the current productive situation of this cluster presents difficulties in this sort of upgrading.

Finally, linkages with the local economy as the third expression of upgrading are found in La Fortuna. We have seen how some small hotels have established a certain tie with local tour operators. This is without a doubt a link with the local economy and therefore an expression of upgrading. Other modes of insertion also involve certain linkages, but the impact is more limited. In San Pedro Sacatepéquez, the factories and larger workshops tend to subcontract certain activities such as washing and serigraphing, but this is limited. In La Palma, we do not know of the existence of this type of link.

The near absence of this mode of upgrading in the Guatemalan and Salvadoran cases can be explained by two factors. First, the small size of the majority of the establishments limits the possibility for subcontracting. If there are moments of having orders that overwhelm the productive capacity of the workshop, they call on other workshops with similar characteristics based on cooperation. Second, external economies of specialization have not developed that would result in the other possibility of upgrading in this third mode.

Thus, in La Fortuna we find a supply of services that could be qualified as differentiated. In this sense, the upgrading of this type of service does not mean moving toward undifferentiated supply, but it does present the need to make supply more visible. In regard to upgrading of phases, we have argued that this makes no sense in the case of tourism. And local linkages can be found in La Fortuna. La Palma offers unique products but with a stagnation in terms of the development of new designs. The artisan nature, pre-Taylorist by definition, means that the upgrading of phases is not pertinent in this case. And local linkages are nonexistent for the two reasons just argued. This same phenomenon takes place in San Pedro Sacatepéquez, where, given the nature of the manufacturing activity, the dimensions of upgrading are found in more well-known manifestations. The product is simple without evidence of evolution toward more complex products, and assembly phases dominate even though local factories have made the leap to incorporating other productive phases.

COMMUNITIES FACING GLOBALIZATION: A SYNTHESIS

With this analysis on the insertion in the global market, we now have all the elements to synthesize the universes that have been studied. We will now highlight the main local dynamics as well as the threats and challenges that globalization presents.

La Fortuna clearly is the most successful case of the three, for two reasons. First, its location in Costa Rica implies a higher level of development than El Salvador and Guatemala. These differences are expressed in terms of levels of welfare. Of the three cases, La Fortuna is the only one where nonpoverty or social integration is universal. Additionally, the differences in terms of educational levels, an important explanatory variable for various processes, are evident. In other words, La Fortuna has benefited from Costa Rican social development that resulted from the nonauthoritarian solution to the crisis of the oligarchy that took place in the country in the late 1940s. Such a situation reminds us that the nation counts. In other words, while our interpretation has centered on the dialectic between the local and the global, this does not mean that the national is no longer important. The case of La Fortuna shows this. In addition, while we are facing a new modernity, the globalized, the inertia of the previous era is still present, and globalization has not meant erasing the old and starting anew. As this locale has benefited from decades of social development in Costa Rica, the higher levels of impoverishment in La Palma and San Pedro Sacatepéquez reflect the exclusionary development models of El Salvador and Guatemala in the previous modernizing decades.

The second explanatory factor of this more optimistic image of La Fortuna relates to the globalized activity of tourism. Here, two elements need to be considered. First, this is one of the most dynamic activities in the global economy in which Costa Rica (again the national enters into play) has been able to carve out an important niche. Second, this type of activity offers possibilities for small businesses that the Fortunans have been able to take advantage of. Thus, it is not strange to find that the labor insertion in the global sector has clear positive effects on the welfare of the households of this locale.

However, this optimism must be tempered with two issues that we consider to be key in the future of La Fortuna. First, collective action is not evident on the horizon. This is due to, again, the national factor and a fundamental element of the Costa Rican model of national modernization inaugurated at the end of the 1940s, based on a passive social citizenship. In other words, the Costa Rican population has enjoyed important social services provided by the state, but these rights were given to them—they were not gained through social struggle. Thus, the accumulation of collective action in this society is deficient. On the other hand, the current dynamism of tourism is such that the Fortunans perceive opportunities for all without the need to organize. Globalization can therefore be accessed individually.

The second issue has to do with institutional limitations due to its condition as a district and not a cantón. This fact is accented here because the country has a strong centralizing tradition. Again, the national and previous modernizations continue to have an impact. Moreover, the institutionality that exists responds to the previous period dominated by agrarian activities. It is not clear how this institutionality can be redefined in order to be functional for tourist dynamics and face the challenges of globalization.

These two latent problems can become critical if nonlocal tourist businesses establish themselves in the area. While this threat is perceived by some of the informants, there is not a collective consciousness about it, and thus the possibility of reacting to this danger, which could be a basis for collective action, does not seem feasible. In other words, the activation of this form of community capital appears to be fundamental for the future of this locale. At the same time, the lack of collective action means that institutional interaction is also limited in addition to the fact that the Fortunans do not control the district resources, thereby permitting greater autonomy within the cantón.

In terms of La Palma, as has been seen, a little more than half of the households have overcome poverty. However, handicraft production has not played a significant role in elevating the welfare of these households. This fact suggests that welfare within this locale depends on a multiplicity of factors in which the globalized activity does not play a key role. However, this community may integrate into globalization through transnational migration, as tends to happen in El Salvador. As we pointed out earlier, there is a positive and significant association between welfare and the receipt of remittances. The lack of significant incidence of the handicraft activity, in terms of contributing to the reduction of poverty, brings us to the second consideration of great importance in the Salvadoran locale.

Probably the main problem affecting the artisan development in La Palma has to do with the type of competition that prevails. Competition is clearly based on imitation and not on design innovation. While the predatory effects of imitation have their limits due to market segmentation, there are other negative consequences. The first is that those who copy tend to crowd out the innovators in the market niches that the latter opened up, through predatory competition that does not incur certain costs (due to the use of nonremunerated family labor, carrying out the activity in the house in order not to incur infrastructure costs, etc.). This form of competition, based on a logic of subsistence, means that the imitators are unable to make the shift into accumulative strategies based on entrepreneurial rationales; additionally, they lower the profits of the innovators. Second, imitation erodes community capital. Faced with the lack of creativity, the process of identity strengthening tends to stagnate. Social control loses vigor and economic life lacks mores. More important, reciprocity is placed in danger. This last point means that cooperation is made more difficult since trust is lacking. This brings about a third negative effect in which collective action is made more problematic.

A third important element in La Palma is of a political-institutional nature. Without a doubt, of the three considered, this locale shows the greatest degree of institutional density. There are multiple institutions, interaction takes place, and leadership in coalitions is even evident. However, the final step of formulating a hegemonic process that incorporates the majority of the population of La Palma is greatly impeded. The reason can be traced to the partisan political polarization that affects this locale, as happens in many Salvadoran municipalities. The confrontation between the FMLN and ARENA has impeded the ability to reach significant agreements, at least for now. Again, the national dimension as well as the past are important, but in this case, and contrary to that of La Fortuna, the impact is negative. While in the previous case, the decades-long national social development was the main explanation of the higher levels of welfare in that locale, in La Palma the aftermath of the war continues to affect local dynamics. In other words, national differences impose themselves on local agreements. Thus, it is not surprising that external actors assume the leadership in interinstitutional coalitions.

The Guatemalan case is the one that presents most clearly the issues related to upgrading in the respective chain. It is also the case where the chain, that of apparel manufacturing, is more clearly configured, with three types of leading firms (retailers, trademark manufacturing, and true industries) and two basic models (simple assembly and integral). According to the Exporters Association in the country, Guatemala is receiving more and more integral package orders since assembly work can be done in other countries. This presents the challenge of upgrading for the San Pedran producers. The recently approved Industrial Property Law decreed by the government due to external pressure makes this imperative. With this law, subcontracted producers of Guatemalan businesses that pirate international apparel trademarks will have significant problems in the near future.

Upgrading in the San Pedran cluster is not impossible. The four large factories demonstrate this, and we have highlighted the case of Villasa, demonstrating the possibilities for upgrading as well as downgrading. The issue is knowing whether this sort of experience can be replicated in San Pedro Sacatepéquez, generating various associated groups of producers. There are three main issues. The first has to do with obtaining integral contracts with firms that are willing to establish long-lasting cooperative relationships with these groups. The lack of a division of labor within this work, with businesses dedicated to the provision of services, makes this difficult, although there are alternative forms to do so through the association. In other words, a mechanism needs to be found that plays the same sort of role that Alvaro Colóm (a key figure in the insertion in globalization) played years ago. However, it is necessary to develop this division of labor, as this would generate external economies of specialization.

The second challenge relates to infrastructure. The integral package involves cutting operations that require very long rooms. This is a major limitation for the vast majority of establishments whose employees, as has been seen, work in their houses. However, the municipal government has lands where an industrial park could be established with adequate warehouses. What is interesting is that for the first time this institution wants to impact the economic development of the community and not just limit itself to providing basic services. The municipal government is trying to obtain a loan with the Central American Bank for Economic Integration to finance this park. If this takes place, San Pedro Sacatepéquez will have overcome one of its main limitations: poor institutionality.

The third challenge, and perhaps the most important, is reversing the deterioration of community capital. The analysis of cohesion in the cluster revealed the lack of cooperation as well as association, in addition to a deep problem of identity erosion. However, the two forms of community capital with poor results, deficient internalization of values and lack of trust, could be revitalized through the activation of the other latent cooperation and association. Thus, bounded solidarity could revitalize reciprocity generating solid trust, thereby permitting cooperation among the owners. However, for this to happen, a collective perception of the need to upgrade needs to emerge as well as a realization that if this does not happen, the vast majority of producers would be excluded from the chain. The dilemma is cooperation or exclusion. Additionally, the incipient institutional dynamic can activate the moralization of economic life, rewarding associative behavior as opposed to individualistic actions. If upgrading is achieved, the San Pedran producers would rediscover the market and could recover a part of the identity lost through subcontracting. In other words, what is at stake is a subtle interaction of the different forms of community capital where the latent ones, upon activation, could revitalize the ones that are already functioning.

COMMUNITIES IN GLOBALIZATION:
AN ANALYTICAL PROPOSAL

In this final section, we move beyond our empirical references and attempt to formulate an analytical proposal that will serve to explain how neighborhood communities, with clusters of small establishments, become inserted in the globalized world.

Small hotel in La Fortuna with a view of the Arenal volcano in the background.
Photo courtesy Heather Burkham.

Main road in the town of La Fortuna.
Photo courtesy Maureen Holland.

Preparing horses for a ride with tourists in the area around La Fortuna.
Photo courtesy Maureen Holland.

Forest canopy in the Arenal volcano Conservation Area in La Fortuna.
Photo courtesy Maureen Holland.

The first point to highlight is that this insertion presents a dialectical play of opportunities and risks. Not everyone shares this idea. The discussion on globalization among skeptics and others can be transferred to this level. On the one hand, there is an optimistic posture that would argue that currently globalization is the only path to growth and therefore represents a world full of opportunities. On the other hand, the skeptical view would point out that globalization by definition is not sustainable, due to its opposition to nationally oriented development, and that therefore it only offers risks. We opt for an intermediate position and consider that the issue should be presented in terms of risks and opportunities offered by globalization. Regarding the risks, we have seen in the preceding chapters how volatility in the markets can not only affect the establishments of the cluster but also impact the welfare of households, putting them in danger of impoverishment. But, on the other hand, through the dynamics of upgrading, globalization clearly offers opportunities that can be taken advantage of in differing degrees and forms. The most important issue, however, is that these risks and opportunities are inseparable.

In this sense, what is interesting is identifying the local dynamics that are at play in neighborhood communities, with clusters of small establishments such as the universes analyzed in this text. Figure 4.1 presents the issues we have identified throughout this text. Additionally, methodological options for analysis are also identified through this diagram, and we start from this point.

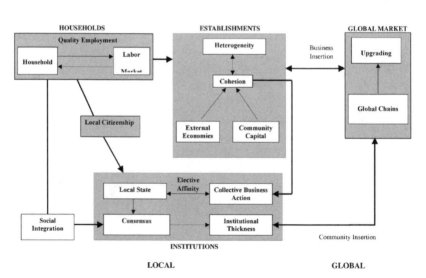

Figure 4.1.   Community Nahual: Local and Global Dynamics and Interactions

A first issue, how to approach the figure, has to do with the dialectic between global and local. One possibility is to enter via the global (the right part of figure 4.1) to study the respective community. This option emphasizes certain issues. The first has to do with a view of the community in terms of its functionality for global accumulation. This means emphasizing the impact of the global on the local, which tends to privilege costs and risks. In other words, there is a tendency to project a passive image of the community facing the pounding force of globalization. The other option is to start from the local side. The emphasis changes, analyzing rather the reaction to the global and tending to focus on opportunities. The image projected tends more toward agency rather than passivity. Obviously, the vast majority of the analyses carried out are a hybrid of these two basic options. But the most important issue is the starting point, since this will emphasize certain elements over others.

If we start on the local side, the other disjuncture within figure 4.1 is where to begin to take apart the complexity of the local dynamics. The diagram identifies three broad social fields in the locale that represent windows for analysis: the cluster of small establishments, the institutions, and the households. Each of these fields implicitly implies diverse issues to be emphasized. The cluster privileges the problems of the businesses and their insertion in the global market, and thus the key issue is competitiveness. This can also be understood from mere economic perspectives and be reformulated in terms of collective efficiency—or cohesion, as we have proposed in this text. Entering from the institutional side focuses on economic governance as the central problem, or whether the existing institutional configuration is able to interact virtuously with the respective cluster in order to obtain a nonspurious insertion in globalization. Finally, households center on the issue of equity in terms of the level of social integration of the domestic unit as well as the labor market but households refer ultimately to the cohesive reproduction of the community itself.

As in the case of the first disjuncture, the majority of analyses try to take into account this complexity, but again the issue is the point of entry because it defines analytical options. Our option in this text, as we argued in the introduction, has been from the local based on the issue of equity. This means that integration into the global market would involve the whole community and not just the most efficient and competitive firms.

Based on this methodological option in the analysis of the three universes, we have identified a series of issues to consider (see table 4.2). We have laid out the three main groups of actors that have been detected in neighborhood community contexts: households, establishments, and institutions. And we confront these with the three main issues that have emerged from our analysis: equity, cohesion in the cluster, and institutional thickness. The cells in the main diagonal are the ones that are analytically the most important. The important thing to keep in mind is that the resulting combination of the interaction of the three main issues is what nurtures, from the local point of view, the possibilities for and types of upgrading. In fact, it brings up the issue of whether the upgrading will be of just a few, the successful entrepreneurs, or of the entire community—in other words, whether actions in the face of globalization lead to individual or collective orientations.

Thus, we reformulate the problem of upgrading in two ways. First, we broaden its application beyond the entrepreneurial arena, including other dimensions, especially social. Second, this broader perspective means that the analysis cannot be reduced to the dynamics within the global market but must also consider the ones that develop within the territory of the community.

The relationship between households and equity presents various issues. The first and most immediate has to do with social integration, which should not be understood in a narrow sense, as the mere satisfaction of material needs, but rather in a broader perspective in terms of participation in community life. This idea will be more fully developed when we relate households to institutions and the topic of local citizenship emerges. For now what is important to highlight is that equity is not merely an ethical problem and thus an issue of options, but rather it refers to community cohesion. In this regard, it can be postulated that cohesive communities, and those not subjected to divisions, are in better condition to face globalization. Obviously, cohesion per se is not enough; otherwise the nonspurious insertion in globalization would be a mere structural effect of this cohesion. The direction this takes will determine the type of community insertion in globalization, which depends on the orientations of the actors involved. In other words, upgrading is a political option but rooted in community cohesion.

The second issue to consider has to do with inequality, which is not the same as disintegration. There can be situations where poverty is limited but there is great inequality due to a high level of differentiation in access

Table 4.2. Matrix of Local-Community Issues in Globalization

	Households	*Establishments*	*Institutions*
Equity	Integration without vulnerability	Nonprecarious employment	Local citizenship
Cohesion of the cluster	Territorial coincidence	External economies and community capital	Elective affinity
Institutional thickness	Consensus	Collective action	Hegemony

to resources. Even though a generalized level of integration exists, these differences generate very divisive dynamics. They tend to break apart the "we" in a community. However, we would postulate that there is a legitimate source of inequality. We are referring to innovation that is able to open new global market niches. In principle, the profit generated is a source of legitimate inequality. But this inequality cannot be limitless and the issue of socialization of profits, after a certain amount of time, is presented so that the barriers of entry in this niche can be overcome. These reflections move us toward the central cell, where the issue is one of innovation. For the moment, what we want to highlight is the tension that can emerge between equity and innovation. The topic of tensions is fundamental and will be taken up again through the final cell, referring to hegemony.

The third issue that emerges from this first cell has to do with vulnerability. This topic questions the dichotomous views of integration and reminds us of the gray zones of integration marked by precariousness. What is important to highlight is that the source of this vulnerability needs to be traced to the insertion in the global market and one of its basic characteristics: its volatility. Here the problem of risk emerges—with the adjective *global*—and it is linked directly to equity through upgrading as it relates to risk management.

The content of the second cell of this first column relates households to the issue of cohesion in the cluster and can be approached from an obvious link: the provision of labor by the households to the establishments. But what interests us is how this provision affects cohesion in the cluster of these economic units. This phenomenon is expressed in terms of external economies and concretely the labor ones that have to do with the existence of an ample supply of qualified labor for the activity in question and its free circulation within the cluster. The possibility that the provision of labor by the households can have an impact as an external economy is due to the fact that the socioterritories of the domestic units coincide with those of cluster. It is precisely in this cell that the territorial peculiarity of the neighborhood community is expressed. This reminds us that in other communities, such as those located in spaces of high urban development, life space and work space do not coincide. In these cases, the cohesion of the cluster is much more problematic since it is more difficult, if not impossible, to mobilize community capital in order to obtain territorial cohesion.

In the cell that relates households with institutional thickness, consensus is the formulation of a local development project that not only gathers together actors and institutions that enter into the dynamic but is able to convoke the majority of the community. In other words, a true political arena that functions as an *agora* without any sort of exclusion, as in the ancient Greek *polis,* should be formed in the community.[12] This project can only be based on consensus. But this is not only a result of political dynamics; there is a material base that can be forgotten, and it has to do with the integration of the households, in its broad sense. Communities that are cohesive are more given to consent; those that are divided, to dissent. In this way, the issue of integration, or even better equity, emerges not only as a result or effect of the global market insertion but also as a condition. Inequitable communities will be less likely to move toward consensus and therefore the institutionality obtained will be thin, thus impacting upgrading. The opposite reasoning can be argued in situations with high levels of integration. Thus, in community contexts equity is also a factor of upgrading.

Moving to the column referring to the establishments, the first issues that emerge have to do with their possible contributions to equity. The key question is nonprecarious employment, which involves various aspects. The first has to do with the dynamic of employment generation. Here the respective cluster should emerge as the main source of employment in the locale. But, second, this employment should not be precarious and should respect minimal labor rights. In regard to this point, the issue is to differentiate between various types of rights. Without a doubt, the most developed proposal is that of Portes (1994), who has postulated the existence of four types of rights: basic (against child labor, physical coercion, and forced labor); civil (association and collective representation); survival (minimum wage, reparations for labor-related accidents, and a regulated work week); and security (against unjustified dismissal, for compensation for retirement, and for reparations to family members in the case of death). Portes proposes that the first two should constitute international standards while the other two should be applied in a flexible manner according to the context. In other words, we are facing a fundamental element of moralization of globalization, and this is not the sole responsibility of multinational firms but also involves local businesses.

This aspect directly relates with a third: how the establishments view labor in terms of competitiveness. If labor is seen simply as a cost, which is precisely what leads to labor precariousness, competitiveness is limited. On the contrary, if the labor force has enough human capital and quality employment, this becomes an effective factor of competitiveness based on the capacity to adapt to market changes and new requirements. The high road of global insertion based on a labor force with high levels of human capital and quality employment is much less spurious than the low road based on a vulnerable labor force and precarious employment. In the case of the low road we face another potential source of tension in the locale. In other words, the class differences exist in the communities even if they are redefined, in two ways: (1) class identities can be redefined in territorial terms, easing possible antagonisms; and (2) the division of labor in small establishments is not very developed. We need to remember that many of these establishments are the fruit of self-employment, and the owners continue to participate directly in the labor process. This presence tends to redefine class relationships between property (not always capital) and labor.

Finally, the nonprecarious employment generated should be accessible to all groups (women, young people, indigenous groups, etc.) who historically have been segregated laborwise. Thus, the issue of labor equity is a question of minimizing not just class differences but also those of other social categories.

The second cell in table 4.2 is the most important in this second column since it affects the essence of cohesion. The first issue is that the fabric of the cluster tends to be heterogeneous since the logics of subsistence and accumulation cross over each other. Obviously, this heterogeneity calls into question cohesion. But before addressing the tendencies that can contribute to this questioning, it is important to reflect on this heterogeneity with several observations. First, given that the historic horizon in which this text has developed is that of globalization, the challenge is how to propitiate logics of accumulation and not subsistence. Second, moralist views with little analytical value on these two logics need to be overcome: subsistence is essentially good and therefore desirable, while accumulation is perverse and objectionable. On the one hand, subsistence can be based on other deep inequities such as gender and/or age that are normally hidden in unremunerated family labor. On the other hand, accumulation does not have to be ruthless, only oriented toward benefit, but can also be embedded in equity in the same way as it was expressed in the previous cell, that is, through nonprecarious labor relations that do not tear apart the community.

Returning to the questioning of cohesion due to the heterogeneity of the cluster's fabric, in chapter 3 we pointed out that the cluster is something more than a group of establishments offering the same good or service and located in the same territory. This is where the issues of external economies and community capital enter in order to understand sectoral and territorial cohesion, respectively.[13] The first of these cohesionary elements presents the following points. First is the need for all types of external economies: specialization, communication and information, and labor. The first of these has been shown to be problematic in the type of contexts that we have analyzed, especially because the clusters show an incipient division of labor among the establishments due to the absence of support services. Second, there is another type of external economy, symbolic in nature, that has to do with whether the cluster is able to erect an image that is recognized in the global world as important. This image transcends the establishments and

becomes part of the community identity. A twofold benefit ensues: reinforcement of community cohesion with an ingredient of identity, and the
constitution of sociocultural community resources that can be a source of
community capital. Third, cohesion implies the generalization of external
economies in that they benefit the maximum number of establishments.
However, what the evidence shows is that the dynamic establishments
make more use of these. And here another tension emerges since cohesion
can, paradoxically, be counterproductive in its effects by accenting the heterogeneity of the socioeconomic fabric.

In terms of socioterritorial cohesion, the key issue is community capital.
We consider that this requires a doubly analytical precision. On the one
hand, we are dealing with sociocultural resources that affect economic behavior, privileging the focus of economic sociology. On the other hand,
this concept refers to individual actions although its sources and effects
can be collective. From this point of view, we posit a process that has to
do with sociocultural resources belonging to the community that are individually appropriated by the owners of the establishments and that can
have cohesionary effects on the cluster. It is the individual appropriation
that constitutes community capital. At the same time, it is important to
highlight the differing modes and the three elements that form this
process. We present the following four sets of triads:

- values/introjection/identity,
- reciprocity/trust/cooperation,
- solidarity/reaction/organization, and
- norms/moralization/innovation.

First, the collective identity of the community generated in the symbolic
external economy can be internalized by the owners to guarantee their
economic identity and thus avoid ruptures in their labor trajectories. Second, networks based on differing types of loans (raw materials, tools, labor, information, etc.) can generate exchanges with sufficient trust due to
their repetition, leading to cooperation. Third, external threats, from the
competitive global jungle, can activate organizational forms among
the owners. And the enforcement of norms can be an incentive to moralize behaviors that favor innovation over imitation. It is important to mention that not all of these forms are active, and this differentiation between
active and latent modes allows for subtle plays in the development of
community capital. Therefore, identity, cooperation, organization, and innovation as the result of the individual appropriation by owners of the establishments can contribute to the territorial cohesion of the cluster.

The final cell of this column puts forth the issue of collective action
among the proprietors of the establishments. This is crucial in that it re-

lates to a scenario of collective rather than individual action. In fact, it is the starting point for the process of institutional thickening oriented toward insertion in globalization. Without this actor, the processes of institutional development can take place but with a different meaning. What is important here is to take into consideration that there are factors that contribute to as well as undermine the formation of this collective actor. Heterogeneity of the cluster, with its diverse rationales, means that interests can be divergent or convergent. In other words, not all the establishments are the same, and not all the owners have common interests. It is through community capital that we find elements that contribute to the constitution of this collective actor. Thus, solidified trust that is able to materialize through cooperation is a start in the collectivization of action.

Also, the moralization of economic behavior means that orientations will not be merely selfish but will also follow upon collective interests. But the other forms of community capital are those that can contribute more positively. Thus, consolidated individual economic identities through the internalization of community values involve attitudes of recognition of community belonging and thus can redirect behavior toward nonindividualistic ends. But it is the reaction to external threats that can truly establish organizational forms among the owners of the establishments. In this regard, it is important to remember what has already been mentioned about risk in terms of vulnerability in the first cell of the matrix. Permanent risk, a result of the volatility of globalized markets, can be a source of reaction in favor of organization. However, despite all these factors that contribute, we can't forget the previously mentioned heterogeneity of the cluster and the corresponding tension that emerges: that which has to do with successful proprietors who do not see the need for or benefit of collective actions.

The final column of table 4.2 brings us to the side of formal collective actors through institutions. The first cell presents a basic issue: that of citizenship, with the adjective *local*. The preeminence that the market obtains in globalization makes citizenship an inescapable issue that also makes relative the market's autonomy. In other words, a market that does not generate and guarantee citizenship, in its different manifestations (civil, political, and social), is deficient. Citizenship allows us to introduce the topics of democracy and equity along with those of efficiency and competitiveness.

Various comments can be made following Marshall's famous typology of different types of citizenship. First, the civil dimension means guaranteeing the right of access to globalization—access through property but also through work and consumption. The latter two elements bring us to the second observation, which has to do with social citizenship and equity. This essentially means that needs are considered rights, as was argued in the second chapter with regard to the issue of vulnerability. Third, political citizenship presents the old problem of participation, but in a new context of decentralization, that involves not only the formulation of demands but also municipal administration as well as accountability of local public authorities. *Local* implies that citizenship cannot involve a rupture of the link with the community but quite the contrary: what is needed is a redefinition of the same in the new globalized context and decentralization. In other words, this new citizenship should involve a new social contract but a community one, and thus the adjective *local*. This contractual process takes place in the political arena, and we have already mentioned the issue of consent. Thus, the symmetry of these two cells in the matrix with respect to the main diagonal is not mere coincidence.

The following cell presents the issue of collective affinity between the dynamics of cohesion of the cluster and institutional thickness. The coincidence of socioterritories is crucial, and it is important to take into account the local state, a key institution, with regard to the defined and assigned territorial competencies. This presents three possible situations. The first is that of coincidence between the socioterritories. This is the most propitious situation to ensure affinity, but it still does not automatically guarantee it; it is still a product of the relationships among the actors and not a mere structural effect. The second situation is when the socioterritory of the cluster is broader than the political-administrative limits of the local state involving more than one municipality. Here we face the emergence of a microregion, induced by globalization, which presents the need for intermunicipal coordination in terms of institutional thickness and affinity. The third situation is when the institutional territory subsumes that of the cluster. In this scenario, two elements are fundamental: the weight of the cluster in the socioeconomic dynamic of the municipality and whether the development of the globalized activity enters into conflict with other interests. The greater the weight of the globalized activity, the better the possibilities for affinity, and the same is true when the potential for conflict is less. This last point suggests the possibility of another tension.

Finally, the last cell, related to hegemony condenses the entire matrix. The question is: What hegemonic project are we talking about? The answer has various components that articulate issues from the various cells. The first to mention is that the objective of this project is the reproduction of the community in globalization. This involves two aspects. First, it implies the reproduction of a community that is not uncohesive and that is able to resist the divisive tendencies that are present in the economic dynamics that propitiate individual orientations and interests. At the same time, it involves the redefinition of this cohesion in the new contexts of globalization and decentralization. This is the idea of local citizenship as a new community contract.

The second component of the answer refers to the means to achieve this community cohesionary objective. Given that the context is globalization, the means are framed within the dynamics of upgrading of the cluster in its different modes (type of product or service, phases, linkages, and a qualitative leap in the activity). But this must coincide with two elements. The cluster of small establishments, with the activity that permits access to the global market, should be as cohesive as possible. We have already mentioned that this cohesion has two components: sectoral through external economies, and territorial through community capital and its different modes. But it also requires elective affinity between the cluster and the institutional formations of the locale.

A third component refers to the actors that assume this hegemonic project, regarding which we have three observations. First, there are two central actors in this dynamic: the proprietors of the establishments of the cluster (involving their formation of a collective actor) and the local state (city council or municipality). Second, it is essential that these two actors not only interact with one another but also do so with other institutions and actors present in the political field of the locale. Finally, they need to obtain the consensus of the population. It is here that the community becomes an actor and faces globalization, through upgrading of the cluster, in a collective manner. This is what guarantees that the upgrading is not just of a few but of the majority.

The possibility of this community protagonism questions those views that limit the actions of the local (as well as regional) to entrepreneurial actions seeking profit differentials between spaces.[14] Despite their invisibility, communities are acting in the global arena.

The reflections in the previous section lead to a general hypothesis: More cohesive communities have better possibilities for ensuring a more sustainable insertion in globalization. This community cohesion depends on a series of factors.

In the first place, it is conditioned by the gains in terms of equity, which involve three aspects: (1) generalized integration without vulnerability; (2) nonprecarious employment, especially in the globalized segment of the local labor market; and (3) the constitution of a local citizenship based on a new community contract in the context of globalization.

Community cohesion also depends on the cohesion of the cluster itself. This implies, first, the predominance of logics of accumulation that tend to minimize the heterogeneity of the economic fabric. This cohesion, however, also involves the development of external economies (the presence of a higher number of them as well as their generalization) as well as the differing modes of community capital. Moreover, the elective affinity between economic and political-institutional dynamics is necessary to reinforce this cohesion.

The third set of processes that determine community cohesion refers to the issue of institutional thickness, which presents three basic issues. The first has to do with obtaining consensus with respect to the insertion in the globalization process articulated with the already-mentioned community contract. The second refers to the need for collective orientations by the actors of the cluster in order to ensure that the institutional thickening is not aborted. Third, the hegemonic character, on a social as well as economic and institutional level, of the local development project is a condition sine qua non of community cohesion.

Thus, as can be appreciated, community cohesion is a product of a complex play of local dynamics in various fields of society. But these are also marked by potential tensions that can influence community cohesion. We have identified some of them. Without attempting to be all-inclusive, we do wish to highlight several of these.

Within the cluster we have identified two such potential tensions: the heterogeneity of the socioeconomic fabric with establishments of simple reproduction, oriented toward subsistence, and those with possibilities for growth oriented toward accumulation. In other words, in the cluster there are potential losers and winners with regard to upgrading—thus the importance that accumulative logics be generalized. If, however, this scenario does not materialize, obviously the upgrading will be of a few. This problem can become worse if the second tension in the cluster develops: the individualist orientation of the successful owners who do not see any advantages in collective action. The prevalence of this type of attitude aborts the dynamic of institutional thickening and thus the possibilities of generating a hegemonic project.

The third tension refers to the problem of elective affinity. The absence of this may bring about the result that only the more dynamic establishments upgrade. If this is the case, the contradictions mentioned in the previous paragraph will be reinforced since the heterogeneity within the cluster will deepen, accenting the individual orientations of the successful owners. But the other scenario can also come about, which would lead to open conflict. We refer to the situation in which the interests favoring globalization enter into contradiction with other actors whose interests are opposed to insertion in the globalized market. This type of situation can lead to a fracturing of the community.

Without a doubt, the main challenge in terms of tensions and contradictions is the relationship between economic and social dynamics. This is the same old song in the history of development, and we have identified three issues.

The first has to do with inequality, which is not the same as disintegration. There may be situations in which poverty is limited but with huge inequalities due to highly differentiated accesses to resources.

These differences, even when integration is generalized, generate dynamics that are uncohesive. They tend to break apart the "we" in the community. However, there is a legitimate source of inequality in contexts such as these. Here we refer to innovation that is able to open up new niches in the global market. But this inequality cannot be unlimited, and this brings up the issue of socializing profits after a certain period of time and overcoming entry barriers for this niche. The key issue is that the innovators not consider themselves simply as successful, suggesting an individualistic attitude (the new rich in the town), but rather as leaders, implying a collective projection redefining economic success in community terms.

The second issue that we have formulated has to do with the high and low roads of labor in terms of competitiveness in the global market—in other words, whether human capital or cheap labor is the best bet. The first option implies considering knowledge and not the traditional means of production as the key resource for entering into globalization. In this regard, conditions need to be created so that the majority of community members have the opportunity to access this resource. On the contrary, the low road leads to class exclusion fracturing the community.

But there is another source of tensions that lead to similar fracturing as that mentioned in the previous paragraph, but whose exclusionary causes are not linked to the ownership of the means of production but to other criteria (gender, ethnicity, age, etc.). In terms of exclusion, this set of possible tensions presents the need to explicitly incorporate these social dimensions, distinct from that of class, in the community contract. In other words, the new local agora should not exclude, as its Greek predecessor did, women, slaves (workers), and foreigners (migrants) as well as other differentiated groups.

These tensions frame our moderately optimistic posture. These types of communities can develop in globalization and winning communities can emerge, but their success is subject to the permanent threats of globalization and internal tensions. The community Nahual can take off again, like the quetzal of Tecún Uman, at the same time hoping that the terrible lance of this new Alvarado, globalization, does not strike it down.

NOTES

1. Gereffi (2001) has recently proposed that with the diffusion of the Internet (commercial as well as among businesses), this distinction is questionable.

2. Not only for our cases, but for all of Central America. The only exception would be the establishment of Intel in Costa Rica as an example of a producer-driven chain (Hershberg and Monge 2000).

3. The reflection is in terms of industrial upgrading. However, it is necessary to broaden this concept to service activities, such as tourism, one of our scenarios, which we will attempt to do later.

4. Sturgeon (2001) has pointed out the problems of false homogenization of this term and has criticized its indiscriminate use in different types of sectors.

5. This dimension has been redefined in terms of opportunities for upgrading in the chain that can be of different natures: functional, in term of vertical integration into the chain, or network (Gereffi et al. 2001).

6. There have already been attempts to do this with tourism (specifically commercial aviation and hotel chains) (Clancy 1998) and agrarian products (Gibbon 2001).

7. The recent repaving of the highway should increase this flow.

8. A recently established artisans' market in the center of town, as well as a new store linked to a project to support small businesses and tourism, coordinated through the national governmental offices of National Commission for Micro and Small Businesses (CONAMYPE) and the Salvadoran Corporation for Tourism (CORSATUR), respectively, has expanded the possibility for direct sales for a number of local artisans.

9. There are no observations on resource upgrading since these sorts of dynamics are not present in our three cases.

10. Augé (1997) defines the organized trip as going to a place of the other while ignoring his or her presence.

11. Some Guatemalan handicrafts, like weavings, have been able to develop in this direction.

12. Upon relating this to equity, we will readdress the idea of political arena.

13. The distinction between the sectoral and territorial is not clear-cut since the territory is an integrator of external economies—in other words, sectoral cohesion (Costa 2001).

14. This proposal is not necessarily made from the neoliberal perspective, as can be seen through the central hypothesis of De Mattos (1994), a non-neoliberal author, has argued that in order to understand territorial changes with the restructuring induced in Latin America by the new accumulative model.

Appendix

This appendix includes three sections. The first has to do with the content of the fieldwork that has been carried out in the three communities. The second refers to the issue of vulnerability, concretely the estimation of the risk of falling below the poverty line. The third issue concerns the linear multiple regression models used in the second chapter.

CASE STUDIES OF ESTABLISHMENTS, INSTITUTIONS, COMMERCIALIZATION, AND HOUSEHOLD SURVEYS

The first data collection was carried out between 1997 and 1998 and included interviews in the respective globalized cluster of the three communities. In La Fortuna (Costa Rica), forty-nine interviews were conducted, forty-eight in La Palma (El Salvador), and fifty in San Pedro Sacatepéquez (Guatemala). Due to the fact that a listing of all the establishments was nonexistent in the locales, initial contacts were carried out through key informants in order to identify new cases through the already interviewed owners until fifty interviews were completed in each locale. The questionnaire included aspects related to the individual traits of the proprietors, basic characteristics of the establishments, socioeconomic relationships within the cluster, and market insertion. During this first period, information concerning institutions directly linked to the respective globalized activity was gathered.

In a second phase of work, carried out in 1999, household surveys were conducted in each of the communities. The universes were reduced to the domestic units located within the urban centers of the locales. With a level of confidence of 1.96 in z scores, with plus/minus 5 percent error and $p = q = 0.5$, the sizes of the surveys were the following: 168 households in La Fortuna, 226 in La Palma, and 270 in San Pedro Sacatepéquez. Simple random samples were used, and households were selected based on the existing cartography from the statistical institutes from each country. The questionnaire included the following modules: sociodemographic, employment, and income.

In this second phase of work, in-depth interviews were also carried out with two types of informants. First, interviews were broadened to include all types of institutions present in the locale, whether or not they had anything directly to do with the globalized activity. Second, people involved in different sorts and parts of the global market insertion were interviewed. This meant that an important number of these interviews were carried out outside the community, in the respective capitals of each country.

METHOD FOR ESTIMATING THE RISK-OF-POVERTY LINE

This estimation seeks to define the zone in the social structure that, while above the poverty line, is marked by vulnerability in which these households run the risk of impoverishment. The lower limit is known, which is precisely the line of poverty, but the upper limit needs to be estimated— in other words, a risk-of-poverty line.

For reasons that have to do with empirical reality concerning what has been done but also for simplification, the exercise carried out has been limited to only one type of risk: unemployment.[1] In this regard, the probability of unemployment has been determined; however, it is not reduced to only open unemployment (the unemployed or new entries into the labor market who are actively seeking employment) but is composed of two other elements: (1) discouraged unemployment—that is, people who in the past actively looked but have stopped doing so even though they are willing to join the labor market; and (2) visible underemployment—that is, people who are employed but work less than a full work week and are willing to work more hours. This last component has been transformed into equivalent unemployment. Thus, the probability[2] of unemployment is a function of composite unemployment that is the result of three phenomena: open unemployment, discouraged unemployment, and equivalent visible underemployment.

Based on the probability of unemployment, the impact on average per capita household income on the domestic units has been estimated for households above the poverty line. In other words, this exercise has involved calculating how much income would diminish if the average number of employed members of a household were to be reduced according to this probability. It would be this reduction, expressed as a certain amount of per capita income that would have to be added to the poverty line[3] (PL) in order to obtain the risk-of-poverty line (RPL).

The algebraic expression is as follows:

RPL = PL + Y – (Y*O2/O1), where
   Y = average per capita income of the households above the poverty line;
   O1 = average number of employed members of nonpoor households without taking into account the probability of composite unemployment;
   O2 = average number of employed members of nonpoor households taking into account this probability.

O2 has been estimated in the following manner:

$$O2 = O1 - \text{composite unemployment}/100$$

It should be remembered that composite unemployment is equal to the sum of the rate of open unemployment plus that of discouraged unemployment and equivalent underemployment.

In this way, the risk zone is made up of those households that are between PL and RPL. This is a proposal that seeks to reduce the normative criteria of the PL in order to reflect the real situation that is faced, without, for example, having the zone of vulnerability calculated as a certain multiple of the PL.

Table A.1 shows the values of each one of these parameters for each of the universes under consideration.

Table A.1. Indicators Used to Calculate the Risk of Poverty

	La Fortuna	La Palma	San Pedro Sacatepéquez
Rate of composite unemployment	29.6	25.7	9.1
Average number of employed members of nonpoor households	1.86	1.93	2.78
Average per capita income in nonpoor households*	75,301.34	1,047.96	730.43
Poverty line*	18,499.40	348.00	403.90
Risk-of-poverty line*	30,502.20	487.70	427.90

*The amounts given are based on the corresponding national currency.

MULTIPLE LINEAR REGRESSIONS

In terms of the regressions in table 2.3, the dependent variable is per capita income, and, as mentioned, it is the indicator used to determine the poverty line. This variable has been transformed using the decimal logarithmic function. Among the dependent variables there are six that are metric. The first is the demographic dependency ratio, defined as the coefficient between the number of household members less than twelve years of age or over sixty-four, divided by the rest. The second reflects the number of years of education of the person designated as the household head of the domestic unit. The four others refer to the number of members of the household who are incorporated in one of the four segments of the labor market: traditional, modern, globalized, and nonlocal. The globalized segment refers to the corresponding activity in each cluster (tourism in La Fortuna, handicrafts in La Palma, and apparel manufacturing in San Pedro Sacatepéquez). The nonlocal segment corresponds to employment outside the respective locale. Modern employment includes the rest of the job positions (in other words, not in the globalized activity or nonlocal) in establishments that employ five or more people; workers in the public sector; or salaried workers that contribute to social security, regardless of the size of the establishment. And the traditional segment picks up the rest of the labor force. Additionally, female-headed household is the only dummy variable, with a value of 1 when the household is headed by a woman.[4]

The next sets of regressions are those in table 2.5. The dependent variable in this case is monthly income of the employed person, which has also been transformed as a decimal logarithm. There are five metric variables. The first is the number of hours worked in the last week. The second and third refer to the age and educational level in years of the employed person. And the fourth and fifth have to do with the number of years employed in the establishment; the squared transformation of this variable relates to the fact that it is expected that the number of years worked slows in its impact on income at a certain point; thus its transformation as a quadratic function. The rest of the variables are dummies. Concerning gender, women have the value of 1. In terms of household headship, the heads of household have the value of 1. Finally, the variables concerning labor segment insertion have been included, and where traditional employment, of lesser importance, has not been taken as an explicit independent variable.[5]

The final group of regressions, found in table 2.6, have to do with the income gaps related to various sociolabor criteria: gender, age (differentiating people younger than twenty-five years of age from the rest); Nicaraguan (for the case of La Fortuna); indigenous (for the case of San

Pedro Sacatepéquez); and class (differentiating among workers, owners, and self-employed whose average income is equal to or above the median income of owners). Regressions in each locale were calculated for the globalized activity and all the other activities considered. The dependent variable is the monthly income of the employed person, transformed using a decimal logarithm. The dependent variables are the respective variable for which we estimate the gap, considered as dummies where the category to be highlighted has a value of 1: women; young people; Nicaraguans; indigenous people; workers. Variables related to human capital are used as controls: educational level and labor experience. These variables have been used in the same way as in the regressions in table 2.5 explained earlier.

NOTES

1. The analytical argument for this choice can be found in the second section of chapter 2.
2. Obviously, this probability is calculated with respect to the economically active population and discouraged unemployed.
3. For calculating the PL, estimates from each of the national statistical institutes for each country were used. These in turn use the methodology of CEPAL.
4. In chapter 2, we mentioned that specific variables for each universe were also processed in the models. In La Fortuna, this included Nicaraguan-headed households (value of 1 for households headed by a Nicaraguan); reception of remittances in La Palma (value of 1 for households that receive remittances); and indigenous household head in San Pedro Sacatepéquez (value of 1 for indigenous-headed households).
5. As in the case of the previous models, other specific variables were also included: Nicaraguans in La Fortuna (value of 1 for Nicaraguan laborers) and indigenous laborers in San Pedro Sacatepéquez (value of 1 for indigenous laborers).

Bibliography

Abraham, A., and J. P. Platteau. 2000. "Participatory Development in the Presence of Endogenous Community Imperfections." Paper presented at the Annual World Bank Conference on Development Economics, Washington, D.C., May 3.

Altenburg, T. 1993. "Estudio sobre efectos multiplicadores de las Zonas Francas de Exportación sobre el desarrollo nacional." Report prepared for the Corporación de la Zona Franca de Exportación.

Altenburg, T., and J. Meyer-Stamer. 1999. "How to Promote Clusters: Policy Experiences from Latin America." World Development 27, no. 9.

Amin, A., and N. Thrift. 1993. "Globalization, Institutional Thickness, and Local Prospects." Revue d'Economie Régional et Urbaine 3.

Amin, S. 1994. "La nouvelle mondialisation capitaliste: Problèmes et perspectives." Alternatives Sud 1, no. 1.

Andrade-Eekhoff, K. 1997. "Asociaciones Salvadoreñas en Los Angeles y las posibilidades de desarrollo en El Salvador." In Migración y desarrollo internacional. Vol. 2, ed. M. Lungo. San Salvador: Fundación Nacional para el Desarrollo (FUNDE).

———. 2001. "Migración y capital social en El Salvador: Reflexiones con respecto al estado de la nación," Report prepared for the Informe de Desarrollo Humano en El Salvador 2001, San Salvador, Programa de Naciones Unidas para el Desarrollo (PNUD).

———. 2002. "Mitos y realidades: Un análisis de la migración internacional de las zonas rurales de El Salvador." Working paper, Proyecto BASIS, San Salvador, Fundación Salvadoreño para el Desarrollo Económico y Social (FUSADES).

Appadurai, A. 1996. Modernity at Large: Cultural Dimensions of Globalization. Minneapolis: University of Minnesota Press.

Arocena, J. 1995. El desarrollo local: Un desafío contemporáneo. Caracas: Nueva Sociedad/CLAEH.

Augé, M. 1996. *Los "no lugares": Espacios del anonimato.* Barcelona: Gedisa.
———. 1997. *L'impossible voyage: Le tourisme et ses images.* Paris: Rivages.
Ayora Díaz, S. I. 2000. "Globalización cultural y medicina: Medicinas locales y medicina cosmopolita en Chiapas." In *Globalización: Una cuestión antropológica,* ed. C. Bueno Castellanos. Mexico City: IESAS/Porrúa.
Bair, B., and G. Gereffi. 1999. "Industrial Upgrading, Networks, and Employment in Global Industries." Paper prepared for Regional Workshop on Decent Work and Global Competition: New Roles for Enterprises and Their Organization, Port-of-Spain, October.
———. 2001. "Local Clusters in Global Chains: The Causes and Consequences of Export Dynamism in Torreon's Blue Jeans Industry." *World Development* 29, no. 11.
Banco Central de Costa Rica. 2001. "Importancia de las empresas de alta tecnología en Costa Rica." Paper presented at the seminar "Industrial Upgrading, Employment, and Equity in Costa Rica: Implications of an Emerging Chain in Electronics," organized by Social Science Research Council (SSRC), FLACSO–Costa Rica, and Corporación de Desarrollo Empresarial y Tecnológico (CODETI), San José, Costa Rica, March 16 and 17.
Bastos, S., and M. Camus. 1998. "La exclusión y el desafío: Estudios sobre segregación étnica y empleo en ciudad de Guatemala." *Debate* 42. Guatemala City: Facultad Latinoamericana de Ciencias Sociales (FLACSO).
Baumeister, E. 1991. "La agricultura centroamericana en los ochenta." *Polémica* 14–15.
Becattini, G. 1992. "El distrito industrial marshalliano como concepto socioeconómico." In *Los distritos industriales y las pequeñas empresas: Distritos industriales y cooperación interempresarial en Italia.* Vol. 1, ed. F. Pyke, G. Becattini, and W. Sengenberger. Madrid: Ministerio de Trabajo y Seguridad Social.
Beck, U. 1998. *La sociedad del riesgo: Hacia una nueva modernidad.* Barcelona: Paidós.
Beck, U., A. Giddens, and S. Lash. 1997. *Modernización reflexiva: Política, tradición, y estética en el orden social moderno.* Madrid: Alianza Universidad.
Benko, G., and A. Lipietz. 1994. *Regiones que ganan: Distritos y redes: Los nuevos paradigmas de la geografía económica.* Valencia: Alfons El Magnanim.
Bordieu, P. 1980. "Le capital social: Notes provisoires." *Actes des Recherches des Sciences Sociales* 31.
Borja, J., and M. Castells. 1997. *Local y global: La gestión de las ciudades en la era de la información.* Madrid: Taurus.
Bulmer-Thomas, V. 1989. *La economía política de Centroamérica desde 1920.* Tegucigalpa: Banco Centroamericano de Integración Económica.
———. 1997. "Introducción." In *El nuevo modelo económico en América Latina: Su efecto en la distribución del ingreso y en la pobreza,* ed. V. Bulmer-Thomas. Mexico City: Fondo de Cultura Económica.
Camagni, R., ed. 1991. *Innovation networks: Spatial perspectives.* London: Belhaven.
Camara Nacional de Turismo (CANATUR). 1998. "Elaboración de estadísticas de turismo en Centroamérica." Unpublished paper.
Carter, M. R., B. L. Barham, and D. Mesbah. 1996. "Agricultural Export Booms and the Rural Poor in Chile, Guatemala and Paraguay." *Latin American Research Review* 31, no. 1.

Castel, R. 1997. *La metamorfosis de la cuestión social: Una crónica delasalariado.* Buenos Aires: Paidós.

Castells, M., and P. Hall. 1994. *Technopoles of the World.* London: Routledge.

Castillo, G. 1990. "Población y migración internacional en la frontera sur de Mexico City: Evolución y cambios." *Revista Mexicana de Sociología* 52, no.1.

Cerny, P. G. 1995. "Globalization and the changing logic of collective action." *International Organization* 49, no. 4.

Clancy, M. 1998. "Commodity Chains, Services and Development: Theory and Preliminary Evidence from the Tourism Industry." *Review of International Political Economy* 5, no.1.

Coleman, J. S. 1988. "Social Capital in the Creation of Human Capital." *American Sociological Review* 94, no.1.

Comaroff, J., and J. Comaroff. 2000. "Millennial Capitalism: First Thoughts on a Second Coming." *Public Culture* 12, no.2.

Comisión Económica para América Latina (CEPAL). 1994. "Centroamérica: El empleo femenino en la industria de la maquila de exportación." Working Paper, Mexico City: CEPAL.

———. 2000. "Uso productivo de las remesas en Centroamérica: Estudio regional." Working Paper, Mexico City, CEPAL.

Cordero, A. ed. 1998. *Cuando las mujeres mandan.* San José: FLASCO.

———. 2000. "Turismo y dinámicas locales: El caso de Flores, El Petén, Guatemala." In *Encuentros inciertos: Globalización y territorios locales en Centroamérica,* ed. J. P. Pérez Sáinz, R. Rivera, A. Cordero, and A. Morales. San José: FLACSO.

Coronil, F. 2000. "Towards a Critique of Globalcentrism: Speculations on Capitalism's Nature." *Public Culture* 12, no. 2.

Costa, M. T. 2001. "As pequenas e médias empresas no desenvolvimiento local: Conceito e experiencias." In *Competitivade e desenvolvimento: Atores e intituicoes locais,* ed. N. A. Araujo and S. Martin. São Paulo: Senac.

Curbelo, J. L., F. Alburqueque, C. A. De Mattos, and J. R. Cuadrado, eds. 1994. *Territorios en transformación: Análisis y propuestas.* Madrid: Consejo Superior de Investigaciones Científicas (CSIC).

Dary Fuentes, C. 1991. *Mujeres tradicionales y nuevos cultivos.* Guatemala City: FLACSO.

Debuyst, F. 1998. "Espaces et identités: Propositions interprétatives." In *Amérique Latine: Espaces de pouvoir et identités collectives,* ed. F. Debuyst and I. Yépez del Castillo. Louvain-la Neuve: Bruylant-Academia.

Del Cid, R. 1992. "Migración interna e internacional en Centroamérica." In *Los procesos migratorios centroamericanos y sus efectos regionales,* ed. R. Casillas. Mexico City: FLACSO.

De Mattos, C. A. 1994. "Nuevas estrategias empresariales y mutaciones empresariales en los procesos de reestructuración en América Latina." In *Territorios en transformación: Análisis y propuestas,* ed. J. L. Curbelo et al. Madrid: CSIC.

De Mattos, C. A., D. Hiernaux Nicolás, and D. Restrepo Botero. 1998. *Globalización y territorio: Impactos y perspectivas.* Santiago: Fondo de Cultura Económica/ Pontificio Universidad Católica de Ecuador (PUCE).

Dicken, P. 1992. *Global Shift: The Internationalization of Economic Activity.* London: Chapman.

Dirección General de Estadística y Censos (DIGESTYC). 1992. *Censos Nacionales: V de Población y IV de Vivienda.* San Salvador: Author.

Doner, R., and E. Hershberg. 1999. "Flexible Production and Political Decentralization in the Developing World: Elective Affinities in the Pursuit of Competitiveness?" *Comparative International Development* 33, no. 1.

Doner, R., and B. R. Schneider. 2000. "Business Associations and Economic Development: Why Some Associations Contribute More Than Others." *Business and Politics.*

Douglas, M., and A. Wildavsky. 1983. *Risk and Culture.* Berkeley: University of California Press.

Dubar, C. 1991. *La socialisation: Construction des identités sociales et professionnelles.* Paris: Colin.

Dundford, M. 1990. "Theories of Regulation." *Society and Space* 8, no. 3.

Durston, J. 1999. "Construyendo capital social comunitario." *Revista de la CEPAL* 69.

Falla, R. 1978. *Quiché rebelde.* Guatemala City: Editorial Universitaria.

Faría, V. 1995. "Social Exclusion and Latin American Analyses of Poverty and Deprivation." In *Social Exclusion: Rhetoric, Reality, Responses,* ed. G. Rodgers, C. Gore, and J. Figuereido. Geneva: International Labor Organization (ILO)/United Nations Development Program (UNDP).

Fine, B. 1999. "The Developmental State Is Dead—Long Live Social Capital?" *Development and Change* 30, no. 1.

Funkhouser, E. 1992a. "Mass Emigration, Remittances, and Economic Adjustment: The Case of El Salvador in the 1980s." In *The Economic Effects of Immigration in Source and Receiving Countries,* ed. R. Freeman and G. Borjas. Chicago: University of Chicago Press.

———. 1992b. "Migration from Managua: Some Recent Evidence." *World Development* 20, no. 8.

Funkhouser, E., and J. P. Pérez Sáinz. 1998. "Ajuste estructural, mercado laboral y pobreza en Centroamérica: Una perspectiva regional." In *Mercado laboral y pobreza en Centroamérica: Ganadores y perdedores del ajuste estructural,* ed. E. Funkhouser and J. P. Pérez Sáinz. San José: SSRC/FLACSO.

Gall, F., ed. 1983. *Diccionario geográfico de Guatemala.* Guatemala City: Instituto Geográfico Nacional.

García Canclini, N. 1999. *La globalización imaginada.* Buenos Aires: Paidós.

Gereffi, G. 1995. "Global Production Systems and Third World Development." In *Global Change, Regional Response: The New International Context of Development,* ed. B. Stallings. Cambridge: Cambridge University Press.

———. 2001. "Beyond the Producer-Driven/Buyer-Driven Dichotomy." *IDS Bulletin* 32, no. 3.

Gereffi, G., and G. Hamilton. 1996. "Commodity Chains and Embedded Networks: The Economic Organization of Global Capitalism." Paper presented at the Annual Meeting of the American Sociological Association, New York, August 16–20.

Gereffi, G., J. Humphrey, R. Kaplinsky, and T. Sturgeon. 2001. "Introduction: Globalisation, Value Chains, and Development." *IDS Bulletin* 32, no. 3.

Gereffi, G., and M. Korzeniewicz. 1994. *Commodity Chains and Global Capitalism.* Westport, Conn.: Praeger.

Gereffi, G., and T. Tam. 1998. "Industrial Upgrading through Organizational Chains: Dynamics of Rent, Learning-by-Doing, and Mobility in the Global Economy." Unpublished paper.

Gibbon, P. 2001. "Agro-Commodity Chains: An Introduction." *IDS Bulletin* 32, no. 3.

Giddens, A. 1994. *Las consecuencias de la modernidad*. Madrid: Alianza.

Granovetter, M. 1985. "Economic Action and Social Structure: The Problem of Embeddedness." *American Sociological Review* 91, no. 3.

———. 1990. "The Old and the New Economic Sociology: A History and an Agenda." In *Beyond the Market Place: Rethinking Economy and Society*, ed. R. Friedland and A. F. Robertson. New York: Aldine de Gruyter.

Gray, J. 1998. *False Dawn*. London: Granta.

Guarnizo, L., and M. P. Smith. 1998. "The Locations of Transnationalism." In *Transnationalism from Below*, ed. M. P. Smith and L. Guarnizo. New Brunswick, N.J.: Transaction.

Guzmán, B. 2001. "The Hispanic Population: Census 2000 Brief." C2KBR/01-3. Washington, D.C.: U.S. Department of Commerce, Bureau of the Census.

Harvey, D. 1989. *The Condition of Postmodernity: An Enquiry into the Origins of Cultural Change*. Cambridge: Blackwell.

Held, D., A. McGrew, D. Goldblatt, and J. Perraton. 1999. *Global Transformations: Politics, Economics, and Culture*. Cambridge: Polity.

Helmsing, B. 2001. "Externalities, Learning, and Governance: Perspectives on Local Economic Development." *Development and Change* 32, no. 2.

Hershberg, E., and J. Monge. 2000. "Upgrading and Equity in Central America: The Case of Intel, Costa Rica." Paper presented at the seminar "Industrial Upgrading, Employment, and Equity in Costa Rica: Implications of an Emerging Chain in Electronics," organized by SSRC, FLACSO–Costa Rica, and CODETI, March 16 and 17.

Hirst, P., and G. Thompson 1996. *Globalization in Question: The International Economy and the Possibilities of Governance*. Cambridge: Polity.

Humphrey, J. 1995. "Industrial Organization in Developing Countries: From Models to Trajectories." *World Development* 23, no. 1.

Humphrey, J., and H. Schmitz. 1998. "Trust and Inter-firm Relations in Developing and Transition Economies." *Journal of Development Studies* 34, no. 4.

———. 2001. "Governance in Global Value Chains." *IDS Bulletin* 32, no. 3.

Ianni, O. 1998. *Teorías de la globalización*. Mexico City: Siglo XXI.

Instituto Centroamericano de Administración de Empresas (INCAE)/Harvard Institute of International Development (HIID). 1999. *Centroamérica en el siglo XXI: Una agenda para la competitividad y el desarrollo sostenible*. Alajuela: Author.

Instituto Latinoamericano y del Caribe de Planificación Económica y Social (ILPES)/Centro de Estudios Urbanos (CEUR). 1999. *Instituciones y actores del desarrollo territorial en el marco de la globalización*. Santiago: Ediciones de la Universidad del Bío-Bío.

Instituto Nacional de Estadística (INE). 1996. *República de Guatemala: Características generales de población y habitación*. Guatemala City: Author.

Itzigsohn, J. 2000. *Developing Poverty: The State, Labor Market Deregulation, and the Informal Sector in Costa Rica and the Dominican Republic*. University Park: Pennsylvania State University Press.

Jessop, B. 1990. "Regulation Theories in Retrospect and Prospect." *Economy and Society* 19, no. 2.

Kaimowitz, D. 1992. "Las exportaciones agrícolas no tradicionales de América Central: Su volumen y estructura." In *Exportaciones agrícolas no tradicionales del Istmo Centroamericano: ¿Promesa o espejismo?* ed. A. B. Mendizábal and J. Weller. Panama City: Comité de Acción para el Desarrollo Económico y Social de América Central (CADESCA)/Programa Regional de Empleo para América Latina y el Caribe (PREALC).

Kaplinsky, R. 2000. "Gaining from Global Value Chains: The Search for the Nth Rent." Paper presented at the seminar "Industrial Upgrading, Employment, and Equity in Costa Rica: Implications of an Emerging Chain in Electronics," organized by SSRC, FLACSO–Costa Rica, and CODETI, March 16 and 17.

Koepke, R., N. Molina, and C. Quinteros. 2000. *Códigos de conducta y monitoreo en la industria de confección: Experiencias internacionales y regionales.* San Salvador: Böll.

Landolt, P. 2001. "Salvadoran Economic Transnationalism: Embedded Strategies for Household Maintenance, Immigrant Incorporation, and Entrepreneurial Expansion." *Global Networks: A Journal of Transnational Affairs* 1, no. 3.

Landolt, P., L. Autler, and S. Baires. 1999. "From *Hermano Lejano* to *Hermano Mayor:* The Dialectics of Salvadoran Transnationalism." *Ethnic and Racial Studies* 22, no. 2.

Lash, S., and J. Urry. 1993. *Economies of Signs and Space: After Organized Capitalism.* London: Sage.

Levitt, P. 2001a. "Transnational Migration: Taking Stock and Future Directions." *Global Networks: A Journal of Transnational Affairs* 1, no. 3.

———. 2001b. *The Transnational Villagers.* Berkeley: University of California Press.

Lin, N. 2001. *Social Capital: A Theory of Social Structure and Action.* Cambridge: Cambridge University Press.

Luhman, N. 1979. *Trust and Power.* Chichester: Wiley.

Mahler, S. J. 1998. "Theoretical and Empirical Contributions: Towards a Research Agenda for Transnationalism." In *Transnationalism from Below,* ed. M. P. Smith and L. Guarnizo. New Brunswick, N.J.: Transaction.

———. 2000. "Migration and Transnational Issues: Recent Trends and Prospects for 2020." *CA2020:* Working Paper, no. 4.

Markusen, A. R. 1994. "Sticky Places in Slippery Space: The Political Economy of Post-War Fast Growth Regions." Working Paper no. 79, Rutgers University. New Brunswick, N.J.: Rutgers University Press.

Martínez, L. 1999. "La nueva ruralidad en Ecuador." *Iconos* 8.

Marx, K. 1975. *El Capital: Crítica de la economía política.* Vol. 1. Madrid: Siglo XXI.

McCormick, D. 1999. "African Enterprise Clusters and Industrialisation: Theory and Reality." *World Development* 27, no. 9.

McGrew, A. G. 1992. "Conceptualizing Global Politics." In *Global Politics: Globalization and the Nation-State,* ed. A. G. McGrew and P. Lewis. Cambridge: Polity.

Mezzera, J. 1987. "Notas sobre la segmentación de los mercados laborales urbanos." Working Paper no. 289. Santiago: PREALC.

Minujin, A. 1998. "Vulnerabilidad y exclusión en América Latina." In *Todos entran: Propuesta para sociedades incluyentes,* ed. E. Bustelo and A. Minujin. Bogotá: UNICEF/Santillana.

Morales, A. 1996. *Los territorios del cuajipal: Frontera y sociedad entre Nicaragua y Costa Rica.* San José: FLACSO.

———. 2000. "El territorio local y la aldea global: La emigración transnacional desde El Sauce." In *Encuentros inciertos: Globalización y territorios locales en Centroamérica,* ed. J. P. Pérez Sáinz, R. Rivera, A. Cordero, and A. Morales. San José: FLACSO.

Morales, A., and C. Castro. 1999. *Inmigración laboral nicaragüense en Costa Rica.* San José: FLACSO/Friedrich Ebert/Instituto Interamericano de Derechos Humanos/La Defensoría de los Habitantes.

Ohmae, K. 1990. *The Borderless World.* New York: HarperCollins.

———. 1995. *The End of the Nation State: The Rise of Regional Economies.* New York: HarperCollins.

Organización International del Trabajo (OIT). 1997. "Aspectos sociales y laborales de las zonas francas industriales del Istmo Centroamericano y República Dominicana: Un marco para el debate." Documento de base, Seminario subregional tripartito sobre aspectos sociales y laborales de las zonas francas industriales, San José, November 25–28.

Orozco, M. 2000. "Latino Hometown Associations as Agents of Development in Latin America." Working Paper, InterAmerican Dialogue, Washington Tomás, Rivera Policy Institute.

Panadero Moya, M., F. Cebrián Abellán, and C. García Martínez, eds. *América Latina: La cuestión regional.* Ciudad Real: Universidad de Castilla–La Mancha.

Pérez-Alemán, P. 2000. "Decentralized Organization and the Transformation of Institutions: Large and Small Firm Networks in Chile and Nicaragua." Paper presented at the Third Meeting of the International Working Group on Subnational Economic Governance in Latin American from a Comparative International Perspective, San Juan, Puerto Rico, August 25–28.

Pérez Sáinz, J. P. 1991. *Informalidad urbana en América Latina: Enfoques, problemáticas, e interrogantes.* Caracas: FLACSO/Nueva Sociedad.

———. 1998. "¿Es necesario aún el concepto de informalidad?" *Perfiles Latinoamericanos* 13.

———. 1999a. "Between the Global and the Local: Community Economies in Central America." In *The Revival of Civil Society: Global and Comparative Perspectives,* ed. Michael Schechter. London: Macmillan.

———. 1999b. *From the Finca to the Maquila: Labor and Capitalist Development in Central America.* Boulder, Colo.: Westview.

———, ed. 1994. *Globalización y fuerza laboral en Centroamérica.* San José: FLACSO.

Pérez Sáinz, J. P., and K. Andrade-Eekhoff. 1998. *Capital social y artesanía en El Salvador.* San Salvador: FLACSO.

———. 1999. "Handicraft Communities in Globalization: Reflections from Salvadorean Experiences." In *Rethinking Globalizations: From Corporate Transnationalism to Local Interventions,* ed. P. S. Anlakh and M. Schechter. London: Macmillan.

Pérez Sáinz, J. P., K. Andrade-Eekhoff, M. Carrera Guerra, and E. Olivares Ferreto. 2001. *Globalización y comunidades en Centroamérica.* San José: FLACSO.

Pérez Sáinz, J. P., S. Bastos, and M. Camus. 1992. . . . *Todito, todito es trabajo: Indíge-nas y empleo en Ciudad de Guatemala.* Guatemala City: FLACSO.

Pérez Sáinz, J. P., and E. Castellanos de Ponciano. 1991. *Mujeres y empleo en Ciudad de Guatemala.* Guatemala City: FLACSO.

Pérez Sáinz, J. P., and A. Cordero. 1994. *Sarchí: Artesanía y capital social.* San José: FLACSO.

Pérez Sáinz, J. P., and A. Leal 1992. "Pequeña empresa, capital social y etnicidad: El caso de San Pedro Sacatepéquez." *Debate* 17. Guatemala City: FLACSO.

Pérez Sáinz, J. P., and R. Menjívar Larín. 1994. "Central American Men and Women in the Urban Informal Sector." *Journal of Latin American Studies* 26, pt. 2.

Pérez Sáinz, J. P., and M. Mora Salas. 2001. "El riesgo de pobreza: Una propuesta analítica desde la evidencia costarricense de los 90." *Estudios Sociológicos* 19, no. 57.

Perraton, J., D. Goldblatt, D. Held, and A. McGrew. 1997. "The Globalisation of Economic Activity." *New Political Economy* 2, no. 2.

Piore, M., and C. Sabel. 1984. *The Second Industrial Divide: Possibilities for Prosperity.* New York: Basic Books.

Platteau, J. F. 2000. *Institutions, Social Norms, and Economic Development.* Amsterdam: Hardwood.

Popkin, E. 1999. "Guatemalan Mayan Migration to Los Angeles: Constructing Transnational Linkages in the Context of the Settlement Process." *Ethnic and Racial Studies* 22, no. 22.

Portes, A. 1994. "When More Can Be Less: Labor Standards, Development, and the Informal Economy." In *Contrapunto: The Informal Sector Debate in Latin Amer-ica,* ed. C. Rakowski. Albany: State University of New York Press.

———. 1995. *En torno a la informalidad: Ensayos sobre teoría y medición de la economía no regulada.* Mexico: Porrúa.

———. 1998. "Social Capital: Its Origins and Applications in Modern Sociology." *American Review of Sociology* 22.

———. 2001. "Introduction: The Debates and Significance of Immigrant Transnationalism." *Global Networks: A Journal of Transnational Affairs* 1, no. 3.

Portes, A., L. E. Guarnizo, and P. Landolt. 1999. "Introduction: Pitfalls and Promise of an Emergent Research Field." *Ethnic and Racial Studies* 22, no. 2.

Portes, A., and P. Landolt. 2000. "Social Capital: Promise and Pitfalls of Its Role in Development." *Journal of Latin American Studies* 32, no. 2.

Portes, A., and J. Sensenbrenner. 1993. "Embeddeness and Immigration: Notes on the Social Determinants of Economic Action." *American Journal of Sociology* 98, no. 6.

Price Waterhouse. 1993. "Actualización del estudio de base sobre las Zona Indus-triales de Procesamiento en Honduras." Unpublished report, Tegucigalpa, Hon-duras.

Pries, L. 2000. "Una nueva cara de la migración globalizada: El surgimiento de nuevos espacios sociales transnacionales y plurilocales." *Trabajo* 3.

Programa de las Naciones Unidas para el Desarrollo. 1999. *Estado de la Región en Desarrollo Humano Sostenible.* San Jose: Author.

Putman, R. 1993. *Making Democracy Work: Civic Traditions in Modern Italy.* Prince-ton, N.J.: Princeton University Press.

Pyke, F., G. Becattini, and W. Sengenberger, eds. 1992. *Los distritos industriales y las pequeñas empresas: Distritos industriales y cooperación interempresarial en Italia.* Vol. 1. Madrid: Ministerio de Trabajo y Seguridad Social.

Pyke, F., and W. Sengenberger, eds. 1993. *Los distritos industriales y las pequeñas empresas.* Vol. 3. Madrid: Ministerio de Trabajo y Seguridad Social.

Quinteros, C. 2000. "Resistiendo creativamente: Actores y acción laboral en las maquilas de ropa en Centroamérica." Paper presented at the seminar "Latin American Labor and Globalization: Trends Following a Decade of Economic Adjustment," organized by the SSRC and FLACSO–Costa Rica, San José, Costa Rica, July 10–11.

Rivera Campos, R. 2000. *La economía salvadoreña al final del siglo: Desafíos para el futuro.* San Salvador: FLACSO.

Roberts, B. 1996. "The Social Context of Citizenship in Latin America." *International Journal of Urban and Regional Research* 20, no. 1.

———. 1998. "Introducción." In *Ciudadanía y política social,* ed. B. Roberts. San José: SSRC/FLACSO.

Robertson, R. 1995. "Glocalization: Time-Space and Homogeneity-Heterogeneity." In *Global Modernities,* ed. M. Featherstone, S. Lash, and R. Robertson. London: Sage.

Robinson, W. 1996. "Globalisation: Nine Theses on Our Epoch." *Race and Class* 38, no. 2.

———. 1997. "Maldesarrollo en América Central: Un estudio sobre globalización y cambio social." *Pensamiento Propio* 5.

Rojas, M., and I. San Román. 1993. "Agricultura de exportación y pequeños productores." *Cuadernos de Ciencias Sociales,* no. 61. San José: FLACSO.

Sabel, C. 1994. "Learning by Monitoring: The Institutions of Economic Development." In *Handbook of Economic Sociology,* ed. N. Smelser. Princeton, N.J.: Princeton University Press.

Sassen, S. 1991. *The Global City: New York, London, Tokyo.* Princeton, N.J.: Princeton University Press.

———. 1996. *Losing Control? Sovereignty in an Age of Globalization.* New York: Columbia University Press.

Schmitz, H. 1995. "Collective Efficiency: Growth Path for Small Scale Industry." *World Development* 31, no. 4.

———. 1999. "Collective Efficiency and Increasing Returns." *Cambridge Journal of Economics* 23.

Schmitz, H., and K. Nadvi. 1999. "Clustering and Industrialization: Introduction." *World Development* 27, no. 9.

Schmitz, H. and P. Knorringa. 1999. "Learning from Global Buyers." Working Paper, no. 110.

Shejtman, A. 1999. "Las dimensiones urbanas del desarrollo rural." *Revista de la CEPAL,* 67.

Sojo, C. 1999. *Democracias con fracturas: Gobernabilidad, reforma económica y transición en Centroamérica.* San José: FLACSO.

Spar, D. 1998. "Attracting High Technology Investment: Intel's Costa Rica Plant." Unpublished paper, Washington, D.C., FIAS.

Storper, M. 2000. "Lived Effects of the Contemporary Economy: Globalization, Inequality, and Consumer Society." *Public Culture* 12, no. 2.

Sturgeon, T. J. 2001. "How Do We Define Value Chains and Production Networks?" *IDS Bulletin* 32, no. 3.

Swedberg, R., and M. Granovetter 1992. "Introduction." In *The Sociology of Economic Life*, ed. M. Granovetter and R. Swedberg. Boulder, Colo.: Westview.

Swyngedouw, E. 1992. "The Mammon Quest: 'Glocalisation,' Interspatial Competition, and the Monetary Order: The Construction of New Scales." In *Cities and Regions in the New Europe: The Global-Local Interplay and Spatial Development Strategies*, ed. M. Dunford and G. Kafkalas. London: Bellhaven.

Tardanico, R., and R. Menjívar, eds. 1997. *Global Restructuring, Employment, and Social Inequality in Urban Latin America*. Miami: North-South Center Press.

Tonnies, F. 1996. *Community and Society*. New Brunswick, N.J.: Transaction.

Torres Rivas, E. 1984. "¿Quién destapó la caja de Pandora?" In *La crisis centroamericana*, ed. D. Camacho and M. Rojas. San José: EDUCA/FLACSO.

———. 1987. "Sobre la teoría de las dos crisis en Centroamérica." In *Centroamérica: La democracia posible*, ed. E. Torres-Rivas. San José: EDUCA/FLACSO.

Touraine, A. 1988. *La parole et le sang: Politique et societé en Amérique Latine*. Paris: Odile Jacob.

Van der Duim, R., J. Caalders, A. Cordero, L. Van Duynen Montijn, and N. Ritsma. 2001. *Developing Sustainable Tourism: The Case of Manuel Antonio and Texel*. Wagenigen: FLACSO/Ecoperation/Buiten/Wagenigen University.

Weller, J. 1992. "Las exportaciones agrícolas no tradicionales en Costa Rica, Honduras, and Panamá: La generación de empleo e ingresos y las perspectivas de los pequeños productores." Working Paper no. 370. Panama City: PREALC.

———. 1993. "La generación de empleo e ingresos en las exportaciones no tradicionales agrícolas: El caso de los pequeños productores en Centroamérica." In *¿Maiz o melón? Las respuestas del agro centroamericano a los cambios de la política económica*. Panama City: PREALC.

———. 1997. "El empleo rural no agropecuario en el Istmo Centroamericano." *Revista de la CEPAL* 62.

Zeitlin, J. 1993. "Distritos industriales y regeneración económica local: Visión general y comentarios." In *Los distritos industriales y las pequeñas empresas*. Vol. 3, ed. F. Pyke and W. Sengenberger. Madrid: Ministerio de Trabajo y Seguridad Social.

Zilberg, E. 1997. "La reubicación de la cultura en la migración internacional salvadoreña." In *Migración y Desarrollo Internacional*. Vol. 2, ed. M. Lungo. San Salvador: FUNDE.

Zilberg, E., and M. Lungo. 1999. "¿Se han vuelto haraganes? Jóvenes salvadoreños, migración e identidades laborales." In *Transformado El Salvador: Migración, Sociedad, y Cultura*, ed. M. Lungo and S. Kandell. San Salvador: FUNDE.

Zucker, L. G. 1986. "Production of Trust: Institutional Sources of Economic Structure, 1840–1920." *Research in Organisational Behaviour* 8.

Index

accountability, 20, 142
actors, 19, 20, 22, 56, 84, 103–5, 113n27, 119, 135; collective, 102, 141; communities as, 4, 31, 143; economic, 23, 45, 88, 109, 144; external or nonlocal, 6, 82, 109, 114n44, 115n45, 130; transnational, 30
apparel industry, 8, 25, 36, 39–41, 106–7, 122, 126, 130
ARENA. *See* National Republican Alliance
Arenal conservation area, 105–6
Arenal volcano, 36–37, 78, 120
Artesanos Unidos. See United Artisans
Association of Artisans and Artists of La Palma (ASAL Palma), 108
associations: business, 5, 103, 105, 107; exporters, 7, 130

Casa de las Artesanías. See House of Crafts
CASART. *See* Salvadoran Chamber of Artisans
citizenship, 30, 43, 63, 109, 128, 141; local, 136, 142–43
clusters, 4, 7, 10, 18, 21, 69–83, 134–36; cohesion of, 77–82, 85, 87–91, 99–102, 131, 136–37, 140, 143–44; heterogeneity in the, 26–27, 64–65, 74–77, 106, 111, 138–40, 141; insertion in market, 120–23 types of, 5–7, 9, 36–41, 70–71
collective action, 69, 80, 82, 98, 109, 113n27, 128–30, *136*, 140–41, 144; and buyer driven chains, 55–56 and community capital, 104
collective efficiency, 5–6, 80, 82, 89, 104, 135
Colom, Alvaro, 41, 107
community: handicraft, 36, 37, 101 (*see also* handicrafts); neighborhood, 3, 9, 13, 63, 87, 90, 135, 137 ; transnational, 29, 30–31, 34n34
community capital, 7, 8, 10, 26, 80, 143 (*see also* social capital, external economies); definition of, 64, 83–84; effects of, 65, 84, 85, 86, 104, 129, 131, 139–41; and external economies, 84–85, 136–37; presence of in universes, 90–92, 96–102; sources of, 85–86, 87–90; social capital, compared with, 8, 83–84
compression of space and time, 2, 13, 15, 17

163

About the Authors

Juan Pablo Pérez Sáinz is a sociologist and has been a researcher with the Facultad Latinoamericana de Ciencias Sociales since 1981. He has worked on topics related to the labor market, poverty, and local economic development. Included among his recent publications are *From the Finca to the Maquila: Labor and Capitalist Development in Central America* (1999) and (together with K. Andrade-Eekhoff, M. Carrera Guerra, and E. Olivares Ferreto) *Globalización y comunidades en Centroamérica* (2001). He lives in San José, Costa Rica.

Katharine E. Andrade-Eekhoff is an urban planner and has been a researcher with the Facultad Latinoamericana de Ciencias Sociales, Programa, since 1995. She works mainly on issues related to social exclusion, labor markets, local development, and international labor migration. Her most recent publication includes (with W. Savenije) *Conviviendo en la orilla: Violencia y exclusión social en el Area Metropolitana de San Salvador* (2003). She lives in San Salvador, El Salvador, with her husband, Oscar, and their three children, Misael, Daniel, and Rebeca.